100
GREAT MINCE RECIPES

100
GREAT MINCE RECIPES

DEALERFIELD

This edition specially printed for Dealerfield Ltd,
Glaisdale Parkway, Glaisdale Drive, Nottingham, NG8 4GA,
by Marshall Cavendish Books, London
(a division of Marshall Cavendish Partworks Ltd).
Copyright © Marshall Cavendish 1996
This edition printed 1996

ISBN 1-85927-104-9
British Library Cataloguing in Publication Data:
A catalogue record for this book is available from the British Library
Printed in Italy

CONTENTS

VERSATILE MINCE

Shaped, stretched, seasoned and sauced, minced meat can be used in a vast range of dishes from all over the world

Minced meat is popular with everyone not only because it is easy to cook but also because it is economical and so many different flavourings can be added to it that a little can be made to go a long way.

All sorts of meat and poultry are suitable for mincing: beef, pork, lamb, chicken, turkey and veal can all be used. Although most meats are now available ready-minced, they remain fresher and more moist if you buy them in whole pieces and mince them yourself at home. With an electric mincer or food processor, it only takes a few minutes to mince your own meat. Do not be afraid to experiment by substituting one kind of meat for another or by mixing two kinds in one recipe.

Lean minced meat has been used for the recipes in this book. It has less fat than ordinary mince and is of higher quality, resulting in a healthier end product.

The recipes show the true versatility of mince as a basis not only for family suppers but also for more formal occasions. From traditional favourites such as shepherd's pie, bolognese sauce and moussaka to new dishes and tastes from every corner of the globe, there are recipes here to inspire and delight everyone.

BURGERS & MEATBALLS

TRADITIONAL HOME-MADE HAMBURGERS ARE ALWAYS
DELICIOUS, BUT WHY NOT RING THE CHANGES BY SERVING THEM IN
DIFFERENT WAYS OR BY MIXING THE MINCE WITH DIFFERENT FLAVOURS?

HAMBURGERS

TO GET THE VERY BEST RESULTS,
BUY RUMP STEAK WHOLE AND MINCE IT
YOURSELF ON THE DAY YOU PLAN
TO MAKE THE BURGERS

SERVES 4 · 30 MINS TO PREPARE
3/4 HR TOTAL TIME · 195 KCAL PER BURGER

450g/1lb minced beef
125g/4oz onions
2 thick slices white bread
1 tbls mixed freshly chopped parsley, chives and
marjoram or 1 tbls dried mixed herbs
1 tsp salt
freshly ground black pepper
1 medium-sized egg
25g/1oz plain flour
25g/1oz dripping or lard
8 buns, baps or soft-crusted rolls

1 Peel the onions and cut into chunks. Mince the steak again, adding the onions to the mincer.

2 Cut the crusts off the bread. Reduce to crumbs using either the large holes on your cheese grater or a liquidizer. Add the breadcrumbs, herbs and seasonings to the mince and onion mixture. Mix well.

3 Break the egg into a jug and beat with a fork. Pour the beaten egg into the mince mixture and mix well until the mince is clinging together.

4 Lightly flour a board. Take 3 tablespoons of the mixture out of the bowl and place on the board. Form into a round cake about 6mm/¼in thick with your hands. Make the rest of the mince mixture into burgers in this way, re-flouring the board as necessary.

5 If preparing in advance, store in a plastic box, placing a sheet of greaseproof between each layer. Cover and chill until required. To cook, spread the dripping on a baking tray and place under a hot grill.

6 When the fat is smoking slightly, place the burgers (as many as can be comfortably accommodated) on the tray. Cook the burgers for 3 minutes each side for rare meat, 4 minutes for medium-rare and 5 minutes for well-done, turning once. Serve at once in soft-crusted rolls with a selection of relishes.

MUSHROOM BURGERS

SERVES 4 · 35 MINS TO PREPARE
1 HR TOTAL TIME · 240 KCAL PER BURGER

3 tbls vegetable oil
1 small onion, chopped
1/2 red pepper, diced
125g/4oz mushrooms,
finely chopped
225g/½lb minced beef
125g/4oz fresh
wholemeal breadcrumbs

1 tsp dried mixed herbs
salt and black pepper
1 egg, beaten
milk, if needed
flour, for dusting

1 Heat 1 tablespoon oil in a frying pan over medium heat and fry the onion and pepper for 6 minutes. Add the mushrooms and cook for a further 2 minutes.

2 Meanwhile, mix the breadcrumbs and mixed herbs in a bowl. Season to taste. Add the vegetables and minced beef and stir. Use the egg to bind the mixture. If necessary, add more breadcrumbs or a little milk to make a stiff mixture that will hold together. Leave to stand for 10 minutes before proceeding.

3 Divide the mixture into four. Lightly flour your hands and form each portion into a burger shape.

4 Brush a griddle with the remaining oil and heat. Cook the burgers for about 3 minutes on each side. If you don't have a griddle, use a frying-pan. Serve hot.

FREEZING

Shape beef mixture round the cheese as in stage 2. Open freeze hamburgers until solid, then wrap individually in foil and pack together in a polythene bag. Seal, label and return to the freezer for up to 6 months. To serve: defrost at room temperature, then proceed from the beginning of stage 3.

VARIATIONS

Grated mature Cheddar cheese or finely shredded Mozzarella may be substituted for the Danish Blue. For a more piquant taste, add a few drops of Tabasco to the minced beef mixture.

SURPRISE HAMBURGERS

SERVES 4
10 MINS TO PREPARE
1 HR 25 MINS TOTAL TIME WITH CHILLING
450 KCAL PER SERVING.

700g/1 1/2lb minced beef
1 small onion, finely grated
1 tbls tomato ketchup
salt and freshly ground black pepper
75g/3oz Danish Blue cheese, mashed
2 tbls vegetable oil

1 In a large bowl, mix together the minced beef, onion and tomato ketchup and season well with salt and pepper. Cover the mixture and refrigerate for 1 hour.

2 Divide the mashed cheese into four portions. Shape each portion into a ball and flatten slightly. Divide the chilled beef mixture into four portions and mould one portion around each ball of cheese. Shape into fairly thick hamburgers, making sure that the cheese is completely enclosed by the meat mixture.

3 Heat the oil in a large frying pan, add the hamburgers and fry for about 5-8 minutes on each side, until they are done to your liking.

4 Remove the hamburgers from the pan with a fish slice, drain them quickly on absorbent kitchen towels and serve at once.

SERVING SUGGESTIONS

Serve in the traditional sesame bun with lettuce, sliced tomato and various relishes or mustard. Alternatively, serve with French fried potatoes, without the bun.

BURGERS WITH SOUR CREAM

SERVES 4 · 10 MINS TO PREPARE
20 MINS TOTAL TIME · 300 KCAL PER SERVING

450g/1lb lean minced beef
1 tbls tomato ketchup
1 tsp Worcestershire sauce
salt and freshly ground black pepper
4 tbls sour cream

1 Heat the grill to high. With a fork, mix the minced beef with the tomato ketchup, Worcestershire sauce and season to taste. Divide the mixture into four even portions and shape into rounds about 20mm/¾in thick.

2 Place a piece of foil on the rack of the grill pan and sprinkle with salt. Place the hamburgers on top. Cook the hamburgers under the grill with the grid 5cm/2in from the heat, for 3-4 minutes on each side, depending on how well done you like them. Serve at once with the sour cream spooned on top of each burger.

BURGERS WITH SPICY BEAN SAUCE

SERVES 4 · 10 MINS TO PREPARE
40 MINS TOTAL TIME · 395 KCAL PER SERVING

450g/1lb minced beef
1 small onion, chopped
1 egg
1 tsp salt
1 tbls vegetable oil
1 garlic clove, crushed
1 red pepper, finely chopped
1 tsp ground cumin
400g/14oz tin baked beans
1 tbls tomato purée
50g/2oz Cheddar cheese, grated

1 Put the minced beef, half the onion, the egg and salt in a bowl and mix together with your fingers. Divide the mixture into four balls, then form each ball into a burger shape. Cover with foil and chill until ready to cook.

2 To make the sauce, heat the oil in a large frying pan. Add the remaining onion, the garlic and red pepper and fry over medium heat for 5 minutes or until soft, stirring frequently. Add the cumin and fry for a further 2 minutes, stirring. Add the baked beans and stir together well. Stir in the tomato purée, then leave the sauce to simmer for about 20 minutes or until thickened.

3 Meanwhile, cook the burgers: heat a large non-stick frying pan over medium heat. Add the burgers and fry for 5–6 minutes on each side or until they are done to your liking. Remove and drain on kitchen towels.

4 To serve, transfer the burgers to plates, top with the spicy bean sauce and sprinkle with grated cheese. Serve at once.

MEXICAN HAMBURGERS

SERVES 4 · 40 MINS TO PREPARE
1½ HRS TOTAL TIME · 380 KCAL PER SERVING

CORN FRITTERS
175g/6oz tinned
  sweetcorn, drained
45ml/3tbls onion, finely
  chopped
I large egg, beaten
50g/2oz flour
½ tsp baking powder
I tsp sugar
½ tsp salt
15g/½ oz butter
50ml/2fl oz milk
oil for griddle or frying pan

HAMBURGERS
450g/Ilb minced
  beef
I tbls parsley, finely
  chopped
I tbls onion, finely
  chopped
salt and freshly ground
  black pepper

1   To make the fritters, place the drained corn, finely chopped onion and beaten egg in a bowl. Mix well. Sift the flour, baking powder, sugar and salt into the bowl. Melt the butter and then pour it into the mixture in the bowl together with the milk and blend it all together.

2   Brush a griddle or iron frying pan with oil, then heat until the oil starts to smoke. To make a fritter, spoon a quarter of the sweetcorn batter on to the griddle or heavy-based frying-pan. Pat the fritter into shape with a spatula. When the underside is firm and cooked, turn with a fish slice and cook until the second side is golden brown. Keep the fritters warm while you make the hamburgers.

3   Heat the grill to high. With a fork, mix the minced beef with the parsley and onion, adding salt and freshly ground black pepper to taste. Shape the mixture into four rounds about 20mm/¾in thick. Place a piece of foil on the rack of the grill pan and sprinkle with salt. Place the hamburgers on top. Cook the hamburgers under the grill, with the grid 5cm/2in from the heat, for 3-5 minutes on each side, depending on whether you like it pink in the centre or well done all the way through.

4   Arrange the corn fritters on a heated serving platter, place a hamburger on top of each, garnish as wished and serve at once.

COOK'S TIPS
For best quality hamburgers, buy your own steak and mince it at home. Do not mince the meat too finely, otherwise the hamburgers lose their succulent crumbly texture. Try not to over-handle the mixture as this tends to toughen the meat.

SPICED PORK SAUSAGES

SERVES 4 · 1 HR TO PREPARE
1¼ HRS TOTAL TIME · 740 KCAL PER SERVING

**700g/1½ lb streaky pork rashers,
  rinds and bones removed**
12 black peppercorns
4 juniper berries
1 tsp dried mixed herbs
¼ tsp dried sage
salt and freshly ground black pepper
65g/2½oz plain flour
1 egg, beaten
vegetable oil, to brush

1 Mince the pork rashers finely. Crush the peppercorns and juniper berries, making sure that the juniper berries are broken into several small pieces. Add to the minced pork with the herbs and ½ teaspoon salt and mix together well.

2 With lightly floured hands, form the mixture into eight sausage shapes. Season the flour with salt and pepper and roll the sausages in it to coat, shaking off any excess. Dip them in beaten egg, then coat again in flour and brush with oil.

3 Heat the grill to medium, and if you have an open wire rack cover it with foil. Grill the sausages for 10-15 minutes, turning them several times until browned on all sides and cooked through. Serve at once.

VEAL & APPLE PATTIES WITH FRESH SAGE

SERVES 6 · 20 MINS TO PREPARE · 1 HR 10 MINS TOTAL TIME
WITH CHILLING · 265 KCAL PER SERVING

**700g/1½lb minced
  veal**
**2 dessert apples, peeled,
  cored and finely
  chopped**
**½ Spanish onion,
  finely chopped**
1 large egg, beaten

**salt and freshly ground
  black pepper**
4 tbls flour
25g/1oz butter
2 tbls olive oil
20 fresh sage leaves
**125ml/8tbls dry
  white wine**

1 In a bowl, combine the minced veal, the apples and the onion. Stir in the beaten egg and season generously with salt and freshly ground black pepper. Shape the mixture into six patties and lay on a tray lined with cling film. Refrigerate for 30 minutes. Sprinkle the flour onto a plate and toss each patty to coat, shaking off the excess flour.

2 In a large frying-pan, heat the butter and olive oil. When the foaming subsides, add the patties. Place eight sage leaves between the patties and sauté over a moderate heat for 4 minutes each side, or until cooked. Remove the patties with a slotted spoon. Drain on kitchen towel and arrange on a heated serving dish. Keep hot.

3 Pour the dry white wine into the fat remaining in the pan. Bring to the boil, scraping the pan with a wooden spoon to mix in any sediment. Boil until the sauce has reduced by one third and strain over the patties. Serve at once, garnished with sage leaves.

ECONOMY PEPPER STEAK

SERVES 4 · 15 MINS TO PREPARE
25 MINS TOTAL TIME· 450 KCAL PER SERVING

700g/1½lb minced beef
juice and finely grated
   zest of 1 large lemon
2 tbls Worcestershire
   sauce
1 large onion, finely
   chopped
salt and freshly ground
   black pepper

2 tbls black pepper
   corns, crushed
25g/1oz margarine
   or butter
1 tbls vegetable oil
2 tbls brandy (optional)
4 tbls single cream

1   Heat oven to 110°C/225°F/gas¹/4. Mix the minced meat in a bowl with 2 tablespoons of the lemon juice, the lemon zest, half the Worcestershire sauce and the chopped onion. Season well with salt and pepper.

2   Divide the mixture into four equal portions and with your hands form into burger shapes about 2cm/¾in thick. Press the crushed peppercorns evenly into both sides of the burgers.

3   Heat the margarine and oil in a large frying-pan. Fry the burgers for about 4 minutes on each side. Remove to a dish and keep hot.

4   Pour the brandy, if using, the remaining lemon juice and Worcestershire sauce into the pan and bring to the boil. Simmer for 2 minutes, stirring to loosen the sediment on the bottom of the pan. Add the cream and heat through, without bringing to the boil. Pour the sauce over the burgers and serve at once.

PORK & APPLE BURGERS

SERVES 4
20 MINS TO PREPARE
1³/4 HRS TOTAL TIME WITH CHILLING
410 KCAL PER SERVING

350g/12oz minced pork
1 onion, finely chopped
1 cooking apple, peeled, cored and grated
2 tsp dried sage
salt and freshly ground black pepper
3 tbls plain flour
a little beaten egg
4 rashers streaky bacon, rinds removed
1 tbls vegetable oil (optional)

1   Mix together in a bowl the minced pork, onion, grated apple and sage. Season to taste with salt and pepper. Using a fork, stir in the flour and a little beaten egg to hold the mixture together. Cover with cling film and refrigerate for about 1 hour.

2   Dip your hands in flour and form the mixture into four round, flat cakes. Handle the mixture lightly as it will be fairly sticky.

3   Fry the bacon until cooked then roll up, secure with cocktail sticks and keep warm. Add a little oil to the bacon fat in the pan, if needed, and fry the burgers, browning them for about 2 minutes on each side. Lower the heat and cook for a further 5 minutes on each side. Top each burger with a bacon roll and serve at once.

BEEF & LEEK PATTIES

SERVES 4 · 20 MINS TO PREPARE
1¹/2 HRS TOTAL TIME WITH CHILLING
380 KCAL PER SERVING

450g/1lb small leeks
450g/1lb minced beef
50g/2oz day-old white
  breadcrumbs
finely grated zest of
  1 lemon
½ tsp ground bay leaves
salt and freshly ground
  black pepper
2 small eggs, lightly
  beaten

plain flour, for coating
25g/1oz butter
1 tbls vegetable oil
4 small thin leeks,
  to garnish

SAUCE
juice of 2 lemons
150ml/¼pt dry cider
150ml/¼pt water

1 Bring a saucepan of salted water to the boil. Add the leeks and cook for 12-15 minutes, until just tender.

2 Meanwhile, put the minced beef in a large bowl and mash well with a wooden spoon to make a smooth, sticky paste. Stir in the bread-crumbs, lemon zest and ground bay leaves.

3 Drain the leeks thor-oughly and chop fine-ly. Drain again on kitchen towel and add to the meat mixture. Season well with salt and pepper and stir in the beaten eggs. Beat well until the mixture is smooth. Cover the bowl with cling film and refriger-ate for at least 30 minutes. Meanwhile, prepare the leek frills for the garnish (see Preparation).

4 To shape the patties, scoop up a heaped tablespoon of the chilled beef mixture. With floured hands, shape into a patty about 1cm/¹/2in thick. Spread the flour out on a plate. Dip the patties in the flour to coat.

5 Heat the butter and oil in a frying-pan with a lid, add the patties and fry over moderate heat for 4-5 min-utes on each side. Add the lemon juice, cider and water to the pan and season with salt and pepper to taste. Bring the sauce to the boil. Lower the heat, cover the pan and sim-mer very gently for 15 minutes.

6 Carefully move the patties to a warmed serving dish. Pour over the sauce and garnish with the leek frills.

PREPARATION
To make leek frills: trim roots and tops from leeks and remove outer leaves. From top of leek make 8 lengthways slits about 6.5 cm/2½ inches long. Plunge the prepared leeks into a bowl of iced water and leave for about 30 minutes until they curl decoratively. Just before serving, remove from the water and pat dry.

WATCHPOINT
The chopped cooked leeks must be dry, or the patty mixture will be soggy.

COOK'S TIPS
Use only the white centre part of the leeks for this dish. Reserve the tough outer leaves to make soup.
Chilling the mixture makes it easier to handle.

SPICY KOFTA KEBABS

QUICK TO MAKE, THESE DELICIOUS KEBABS
WILL TEMPT EVERYONE TO THE TABLE

SERVES 4 · 20 MINS TO PREPARE
30 MINS TOTAL TIME · 395 KCAL PER SERVING

700g/1½ lb lean minced lamb
1 tbls garam masala
1 tsp ground coriander
½ tsp ground cumin
2-3 garlic cloves, crushed
½ tsp ground ginger
1 onion, grated
2 tbls lime juice
salt and freshly ground black pepper
3 tbls choppped coriander
coriander sprigs and lime wedges, to garnish

1 Mix all the ingredients except the garnish together in a large bowl. Divide the mixture into eight and shape each portion into a sausage shape. Spear two on each wooden skewer.

2 Heat the grill to medium high. Place the skewers under the grill for 3 minutes each side until browned all over and cooked through. Transfer the cooked skewers to a warmed serving plate.

3 Skim the fat from the juices and season to taste. Pour over the kebabs and serve on a bed of lettuce garnished with coriander sprigs and lime wedges.

WHAT TO DRINK

Coriander is a difficult flavour to match with wine, but a dry country red from Greece would fit the bill.

SPICED KEBABS

SERVES 6 · 10 MINS TO PREPARE · 1 HR 20 MINS TOTAL TIME
WITH CHILLING · 235 KCAL PER SERVING

700g/1¹/2lb minced beef
1 tbls tomato purée
1 tsp ground mixed spice
1 tbls plain flour
1 onion, grated
1 clove garlic, crushed
4 tbls lemon juice
salt and freshly ground black pepper

1 Put all the ingredients in a large bowl and mix together with your hands until well combined.

2 Divide the mixture into six and shape each piece into a sausage shape about 7.5cm/3in long, packing the mixture together firmly.

3 Cover and refrigerate the kebabs for at least 1 hour. Heat the grill to high. Carefully thread each kebab lengthways on to an oiled long skewer. Place the skewers on the heated grill pan.

4 Grill for about 10 minutes, turning from time to time, until cooked through. Serve at once.

COOK'S TIP
If you haven't time to refrigerate the mixture for 1-2 hours, put the uncooked kebabs into the freezer for 30 minutes. Chilling makes them easier to thread on to skewers.

BEEFBALL & APRICOT KEBABS

SERVES 4 · 30 MINS TO PREPARE
55 MINS TOTAL TIME. · 525 KCAL PER SERVING

450g/1lb minced beef
1 small onion, grated
25g/1oz fresh white
breadcrumbs
¹/2 tsp ground ginger
¹/4 tsp dried thyme
¹/2 tsp salt
¹/4 tsp freshly
ground black pepper
1 egg, lightly beaten
6 rashers streaky bacon
6 large dried apricots, halved

BARBECUE SAUCE
3 tbls wine vinegar
2 tbls dark soft brown
sugar
2 tbls tomato ketchup
2 tbls fruit chutney
2 tsp cornflour
2 tsp soy sauce
275ml/¹/2pt water
salt and freshly ground
black pepper

1 Mix together the beef, onion, breadcrumbs, ginger, thyme and salt and pepper. Add the egg, then mix with your hands until combined. Shape into 16 balls.

2 Remove the rind from the bacon rashers and cut each one in half, then wrap each one around an apricot half. Thread the meatballs and apricots in bacon alternately on to four skewers allowing four meatballs and three apricots in bacon for each. Heat the grill to high. Grill the kebabs for 7-10 minutes, turning them over frequently until browned and cooked through.

3 Meanwhile, make the barbecue sauce: put all the ingredients into a saucepan and bring to the boil, stirring constantly. Boil for 2 minutes. Serve the kebabs at once, with the sauce poured over.

BEEF & COCONUT PATTIES

SERVES 4 · 40 MINS TO PREPARE
1 HR TOTAL TIME · 700 KCAL PER SERVING

225g/½lb desiccated coconut
450g/1lb minced beef
2 garlic cloves, crushed
¹/2tsp blachan (dried shrimp paste) (optional)
2 tsp ground coriander
1 tsp ground cumin
¹/2 tsp ground ginger
2 eggs, lightly beaten
vegetable oil, for deep-frying
fresh coriander and onion rings, to garnish

BATTER
125g/4oz flour
150ml/¼pt water
2 small eggs, lightly beaten

1 Put the coconut into a bowl and moisten with about 8 tablespoons of boiling water. Then stir in all the remaining patty ingredients and beat until they are smooth and well blended. Using your hands, shape the mixture into about 12 patty shapes. Chill while you make the batter.

2 To make the batter, beat the flour, water and egg together to make a light, thin batter. Dip each patty in turn in the batter to coat them thoroughly. Set aside.

3 Fill a deep, heavy-based pan about one third full of vegetable oil and heat until the oil is very hot (180°C/350°F). Carefully lower the patties into the oil, a few at a time, and fry until they are crisp and golden brown, about 10 minutes. Using a slotted spoon, transfer the patties to kitchen towels, then keep hot until you serve.

4 Serve at once garnished with fresh coriander leaves and raw onion rings.

BITOKS À LA RUSSE

SERVES 4 · 40 MINS TO PREPARE
1 HR 10 MINS TOTAL TIME · 735 KCAL PER SERVING

125g/4oz fresh white breadcrumbs
3-4 tbls milk
450g/1lb minced beef
125g/4oz butter, softened
generous pinch of paprika
salt and freshly ground black pepper
2 tbls flour
1 large egg
2 tbls olive oil
1 large Spanish onion, finely chopped

SAUCE
4 tbls beef stock
3 tbls sour cream
15g/¹/2oz butter

1 Soak half the bread-crumbs in the milk for 5 minutes. Squeeze out any excess milk. Combine the soaked breadcrumbs with the minced beef, 50g/2oz of the butter and the paprika. Season the mixture with salt and pepper to taste, and blend thoroughly with a wooden spoon. Divide into four balls.

2 Put the flour in a shallow dish and season with salt and pepper. Beat the egg lightly. Put the remaining breadcrumbs in another shallow dish. Flatten the meat balls into round patties. Toss each patty in the seasoned flour, then dip in the lightly beaten egg and toss in the breadcrumbs, patting the coating on firmly.

3 In a large frying-pan heat 1 tablespoon olive oil with 25g/1oz butter and sauté the patties slowly for 5-7 minutes on each side, or until golden brown and just cooked through. Transfer to a heated serving platter and keep warm.

4 Meanwhile, in a small frying pan heat the remaining butter and oil and sauté the finely chopped onion until soft and a deep golden colour. Remove with a slotted spoon and keep warm.

5 To make the sauce: drain off any excess fat from the pan in which the patties were cooked and pour in the beef stock. Bring to the boil, scraping the sides and bottom of the pan with a wooden spoon to dislodge any crusty bits. Stir in the sour cream. Bring quickly to boiling point again and remove from the heat. Finally, beat in the butter, a small piece at a time.

6 To serve, garnish each patty with a teaspoon of sautéed onion. Serve at once with the cream sauce poured over the top.

CHICKEN & RATATOUILLE PATTIES

SERVES 4 · 30 MINS TO PREPARE
1¹/₂ HRS TOTAL TIME WITH COOLING AND CHILLING
345 KCAL PER SERVING

450g/1lb minced chicken
150ml/¹/₄pt ratatouille,
   homemade or tinned
1 garlic clove, finely
   chopped or crushed
¹/₂ tsp dried basil
salt and freshly ground
   black pepper
50g/2oz ham,
   cubed
50g/2oz cooked white or
   brown rice (25g/1oz
   raw rice)
2 tbls chopped
   parsley
1 tbls beaten egg
flour, for coating
2 tbls oil
40g/1½oz butter
150ml/¹/₄pt strong
   chicken stock
2 tsp tomato purée
creamed chopped
   spinach, to serve

1 Put the ratatouille in a saucepan and sprinkle with the garlic. Add the basil and season lightly with salt to taste. Simmer gently for 5 minutes, or until most of the liquid has disappeared, stirring often. Remove from the heat and let cool.

2 Combine the chicken, ham and rice and put them through a mincer. Mix in the ratatouille and parsley. Season with salt and pepper to taste and work in the egg.

3 With floured hands, shape the mixture into eight patties, about 15mm/¹/₂in thick. Refrigerate for 30 minutes to firm up.

4 Heat the oil and 2 tablespoons butter in a heavy frying-pan large enough to hold the patties in one layer. Coat the patties with flour and fry them for 2 minutes on each side over a high heat, then reduce the heat and cook turning once, for 10 minutes.

5 Remove the patties from the pan with a fish slice and keep warm. Add the stock and tomato purée to the pan. Raise the heat and boil, stirring constantly, until the sauce is reduced to about 5 tablespoons. Whisk in the remaining butter.

6 Serve the patties on a bed of creamed spinach with a little sauce poured over each.

FRIKADELLER

FRIKADELLER, THE EGG-SHAPED
DANISH VERSION OF MEATBALLS,
ARE ONE OF DENMARK'S MOST
POPULAR DISHES. MOST DANISH
FAMILIES EAT THEM AT LEAST ONCE A WEEK

SERVES 4 · 20 MINS TO PREPARE
30 MINS TOTAL TIME · 580 KCAL PER SERVING

450g/1lb minced pork
2 tbls plain flour
150ml/^{1}/4pt milk
1 egg, beaten
1 small onion, grated or minced
^{1}/2 tsp ground allspice (optional)
salt
freshly ground black pepper
125g/4oz unsalted butter, melted

1 Heat oven to 130°C/250°F/gas^1/2. Put the minced pork in a large bowl, sprinkle in the flour and very gradually stir in the milk to mix thoroughly. Stir in the egg, onion and allspice, if using, and season with salt and freshly ground black pepper to taste.

2 Heat half the melted butter in a frying pan. Dip a tablespoon in the remaining butter and scoop up a heaped spoonful of the pork mixture.

3 Shape and fry the frikadeller over moderate heat for 5 minutes on each side, adding more butter to the frying pan as needed and dipping the spoon in the butter each time you scoop up the pork mixture. Transfer the cooked frikadeller to a warmed serving dish and keep hot while you fry the remainder. Serve hot.

GAMMON & PORK BALLS

SERVES 4 · 20 MINS TO PREPARE
30 MINS TOTAL TIME · 275 KCAL PER SERVING.

250g/9oz lean gammon, rinds removed, finely minced
250g/9oz lean pork, finely minced
1 small onion, finely minced
50g/2oz fresh white breadcrumbs
1 tsp English mustard
^{1}/2 tsp ground coriander
salt and freshly ground black pepper
1 tbls vegetable oil
large pinch of finely grated orange zest
juice of 2 oranges
orange twists and watercress sprig, to garnish

1 Put the gammon, pork and onion into a bowl. Add the breadcrumbs, mustard, coriander and salt and pepper to taste, and mix thoroughly with a fork. Using floured hands to prevent the mixture from sticking to them, carefully shape the mixture into about 24 small balls.

2 Heat the oil in a frying pan, add the prepared balls and fry over moderate heat for 6-8 minutes, turning frequently, until browned all over. Transfer to a plate, drain off all the fat from the pan, then replace the balls in the pan.

3 Mix the orange zest and juice together and pour into the pan. Bring to the boil, then boil rapidly for 1-2 minutes until the liquid is reduced by half, shaking the pan frequently to prevent the meatballs from sticking to the pan. Serve the meatballs in a ring of rice or piped potatoes with the sauce poured over. Garnish with orange twists and a sprig of watercress.

EGG & LEMON MEATBALLS

SERVES 4 · 25 MINS TO PREPARE
1HR .10 MINS TOTAL TIME
595 KCAL PER SERVING

700g/1½lb lean minced beef
2 slices bread, crusts removed
1 large onion, grated
2 eggs, beaten
salt and freshly ground
black pepper
425ml/¾pt water
8 tbls lemon juice
1 tbls sugar
3 egg yolks
plain flour, for coating
sweet paprika, to garnish

1 Put the bread in a small bowl, cover with cold water and leave to stand for about 10 minutes. Meanwhile, put the minced beef in a bowl. Add the grated onion and beaten eggs and stir well with a wooden spoon to mix and remove any lumps in the mince.

2 Squeeze the soaked bread with your hands to extract as much water as possible, then add to the beef mixture with salt and pepper to taste. Mix everything together with your hands.

3 Divide the beef mixture into 20 portions and roll into balls with floured hands. Pour the measured water into a large saucepan. Add the lemon juice, sugar and salt and pepper to taste and bring to the boil.

4 Add the meatballs to the pan a few at a time. Bring back to the boil, lower the heat, cover and simmer very gently for 40 minutes. Taste the cooking liquid and add more lemon juice or sugar if necessary.

5 Beat the egg yolks in a bowl. Remove the pan from the heat and, using a large metal spoon, very gradually trickle the hot liquid on to the egg yolks, beating all the time.

6 When most of the liquid from the pan has been added to the yolks, return the mixture to the pan and, off the heat, carefully turn the meatballs to coat them thoroughly in the sauce. Serve at once.

SERVING IDEAS
Serve the meatballs in soup bowls as there is a lot of sauce, accompanied by plenty of mashed potatoes to soak the sauce up.

COOK'S TIPS
The average lemon contains about 2 tablespoons juice, so you will need about 4 lemons for this recipe.
The flavour of the sauce should be sweet and sour. Adjust it accordingly, adding more lemon juice for extra sharpness or a pinch of sugar if it is too sour.

WATCHPOINTS
Add the hot liquid to the egg yolks very slowly or the mixture will curdle.
If you need to reheat the dish once the egg yolks are incorporated, do so very gently, over very low heat, and on no account allow the mixture to boil.

GERMAN MEATBALLS

SERVES 4 · 30 MINS TO PREPARE
1 HR TOTAL TIME · 435 KCAL PER SERVING

450g/1lb minced beef
4 tbls fresh breadcrumbs
½ tsp dried marjoram
1 tbls chopped parsley
salt and pepper
4 tbls milk
1 large egg, lightly beaten
25g/1oz butter
1 tbls oil
1 small onion, chopped
125g/4oz mushrooms, quartered
275ml/½pt beef
**   consommé**
150ml/¼pt sour cream
fresh herbs, to garnish

1 Put the meat in a bowl and mix in the breadcrumbs and herbs. Season generously with salt and pepper, then stir in the milk and egg. With wet hands, shape the mixture into 24 balls.

2 Heat the butter and oil in a large frying-pan. Brown the meatballs over medium heat for 4 minutes, shaking the pan so that they colour evenly. Transfer them to a plate with a slotted spoon and keep warm.

3 Put the onion and mushrooms in the pan and fry for 5 minutes stirring occasionally until just beginning to soften. Stir in the consommé and return the meatballs to the pan. Simmer, uncovered, for 25 minutes until the meatballs are cooked and the sauce has reduced by half, turning the meatballs frequently.

4 Transfer the meatballs to a serving dish using a slotted spoon. Stir the sour cream into the sauce: do not let it boil. Pour the sauce over the meatballs and serve hot, garnished with fresh herbs.

PORK BALLS WITH GINGER

SERVES 4 · 30 MINS TO PREPARE · 1 HR TOTAL TIME
WITH SOAKING · 550 KCAL PER SERVING

700g/1½ lb minced pork
2.5cm/1in piece of fresh root ginger, peeled and finely chopped
4 water chestnuts, drained and finely chopped
1 egg
1 tsp salt
1 tbls soya sauce
5 tbls cornflour
1 tsp sugar
8 dried mushrooms, soaked in cold water for 30 minutes
50g/2oz bean sprouts
1 green pepper, deseeded and chopped
8 tbls vegetable oil

SAUCE
5 tbls wine vinegar
5 tbls dry sherry
2 tbls sugar
2 tbls tomato purée
1 tbls soya sauce
salt and freshly ground black pepper
1 tsp cornflour, mixed to a paste with 2 tbls water

1 Combine the pork, ginger, water chestnuts, egg, salt, soya sauce, 2 tablespoons of cornflour and sugar thoroughly. Shape into 12 balls. Put the remaining cornflour on a plate and roll the balls in it to coat them.

2 Remove the mushrooms from the water and squeeze dry. Remove and discard the stalks. Cut them, and the peppers, into strips.

3 Heat 6 tablespoons of the oil in a frying pan. When it is hot, reduce the heat to moderately low and add the pork balls. Fry, turning frequently, for 15 minutes or until they are cooked through and crisp. Transfer to a warmed dish. Cover and keep hot.

4 Combine all the sauce ingredients together, except the cornflour.

5 Pour off and discard the oil in the pan. Rinse and wipe the pan dry, and return it to high heat for 30 seconds. Add the remaining oil and reduce the heat to moderate. Add the vegetables and stir-fry for 3 minutes. Pour over the sauce and stir-fry for a further 3 minutes.

6 Stir in the cornflour mixture and stir-fry until the sauce thickens. Pour over the pork balls and serve.

HAM & BEEF PATTIES WITH ANCHOVY BUTTER

SERVES 4 · 30 MINS TO PREPARE
3/4 HR TOTAL TIME · 450 KCAL PER SERVING

450g/1lb minced beef
salt and freshly ground black pepper
Dijon mustard
4 thin slices cooked ham, about 125g/4oz
25g/1oz butter
2 tbls olive oil
4 spring onion flowers, to garnish

ANCHOVY BUTTER
4 tinned anchovies, drained
2 tbls softened butter
freshly ground black pepper

1 In a bowl, season the minced beef generously with salt and freshly ground black pepper. Wet your hands and form the meat into eight even-sized oval patties.

2 Spread each of four patties with 2 teaspoons Dijon mustard, then place 1 slice of cooked ham over the mustard on each patty. Trim the ham to fit neatly on the patty and arrange the trimmings over each trimmed slice. Top each ham patty with one of the remaining patties, pressing firmly and pinching the meat together round the sides to enclose the ham.

3 Select a frying-pan large enough to take the four patties comfortably in one layer. Heat the butter and olive oil. When the foaming subsides, place the patties side by side in the pan and cook over a moderate heat for 3-4 minutes each side, or until cooked but still lightly pink in the middle, turning with a spatula.

4 Meanwhile, make the anchovy butter. Put the drained anchovy fillets in a mortar and pound them until soft with a pestle, gradually working in the butter until the mixture is well blended. Season with freshly ground black pepper to taste.

5 Remove the patties from the pan and drain them well on kitchen towels to absorb any excess fat.

6 Arrange on a heated serving platter. Divide the anchovy butter between the patties, spooning it on top of each. Garnish each patty with a spring onion flower (see Preparation *page 15*) and serve at once.

MEATBALL CASSEROLE

SERVES 4
45 MINS TO PREPARE
1 1/4 HRS TOTAL TIME
590 KCAL PER SERVING

**700g/1 1/2lb finely
  minced lean beef
1 onion, grated
4 tbls fresh white
  breadcrumbs
1 egg, beaten
2 tbls tomato purée
1 tsp Worcestershire
  sauce
salt and freshly ground
  black pepper
40g/1 1/2oz plain flour
3 tbls vegetable oil
1 onion, chopped
450g/1lb potatoes, cut
  into 2.5 cm/1in chunks
3 carrots, sliced
425ml/3/4pt beef stock
400g/14oz tin tomatoes
3 courgettes, cut into
  2cm/3/4in pieces
1/2 tsp dried thyme
1 bay leaf**

1 Put the minced beef in a bowl together with the grated onion, breadcrumbs, egg, tomato purée, Worcestershire sauce, 1½ teaspoons salt and plenty of pepper. Mix well until thoroughly blended, then divide the mixture into 20 pieces. With floured hands to prevent sticking, roll each piece into a ball.

2 Spread the flour out on a flat plate and roll the meatballs in it until they are evenly coated, shaking off and reserving the excess flour.

3 Heat 2 tablespoons of the oil in a large flameproof casserole. Add the meatballs a few at a time and fry over moderate heat for 5-6 minutes until well browned all over, turning frequently. Remove and drain on kitchen towels. Continue until all the meatballs are browned.

4 Heat the remaining oil in the casserole, add the onion, potatoes and carrots and fry for 4-5 minutes, stirring constantly. Stir in the reserved flour, then the stock and tomatoes with their juice. Bring to the boil, stirring and scraping any sediment off the base and sides of the casserole. Add the courgettes, thyme, bay leaf and salt and pepper to taste, lower the heat, cover and simmer gently for 15 minutes.

5 Return the meatballs to the casserole and stir gently to cover them with sauce. Cover and simmer for a further 25 minutes. Serve at once, straight from the casserole. Serve in soup plates with boiled noodles or French bread, and a salad.

MEATBALL SALAD

SERVES 4 · 30 MINS TO PREPARE
1 HR TOTAL TIME WITH MARINATING
AND COOLING · 300 KCAL PER SERVING

450g/1lb lean minced beef
4 large button mushrooms, cut into quarters
2 tbls grated onion
2 tbls tomato relish or chutney
¼ tsp dried marjoram or mixed herbs
50g/2oz fresh white breadcrumbs
1 egg, beaten
2 tomatoes, cut into eighths
1 small round lettuce, shredded
1 green pepper, deseeded and sliced into rings
½ cucumber, thinly sliced
vegetable oil, for brushing

MARINADE
3 tbls vegetable oil
1 tbls lemon juice
1 garlic clove, crushed
salt and freshly ground black pepper

1 To make the marinade, combine the oil, lemon juice and garlic in a bowl. Season to taste with salt and pepper. Add the mushrooms, toss thoroughly and leave them to marinate for at least 1 hour.

2 Meanwhile, heat the grill to high. Mix together the minced beef, grated onion, tomato relish, herbs and breadcrumbs. Season with salt and pepper to taste and add enough beaten egg to bind the mixture (about 1 tablespoon).

3 Divide the meat mixture into 16 portions and form each into a ball. Brush with oil and place on the rack in the grill pan.

4 Grill the meat balls for 15 minutes, turning as necessary, until brown and cooked through. Drain on kitchen towels, then set aside to cool for 30 minutes.

5 Arrange the lettuce, green pepper and cucumber on a serving plate. Using a slotted spoon, transfer the mushrooms from the marinade to a plate. Thread the meat balls, tomatoes and mushrooms on cocktail sticks and arrange next to the salad. Serve at once.

MEXICAN DIPPERS

SERVES 12 AS A STARTER
25 MINS TO PREPARE
50 MINS TOTAL TIME
370 KCAL PER SERVING

900g/2lb minced beef
2 onions, chopped
175g/6oz fresh white
   breadcrumbs
2 eggs, beaten
1 tsp chilli powder
salt and freshly ground
   black pepper
vegetable oil, for frying
halved cherry tomatoes and
   sprigs of dill, to garnish
taco chips and crisps, to serve

DIP
250g/9oz full-fat soft cheese with
   garlic and herbs
450ml/¾pt sour cream
6 tomatoes, skinned,
   seeded and finely chopped
2 tbls tomato chilli relish
1 tbls tomato ketchup
1 tbls chopped parsley

1 To make the dip, place the cheese in a large bowl and beat with a wooden spoon until slightly softened.

2 Mix in the sour cream, tomatoes, relish, ketchup, parsley and salt and pepper to taste.

3 To make the meatballs: in a large bowl, combine the beef, onions, breadcrumbs, eggs and chilli powder and season with salt and pepper to taste. Mix well then divide and shape the meat into about 45 small balls about 2.5cm/1in in diameter.

4 To cook the meatballs, heat the oil in a frying-pan, add the prepared balls and fry over moderate heat for 6-8 minutes, turning frequently, until browned all over. Transfer the meatballs to a plate with a slotted spoon.

5 To serve, decant the cheese dip to small serving dishes, garnish with the cherry tomatoes and dill sprigs and serve with the meatballs, taco chips and crisps.

DIPPERS FOR DIPS
A selection of foods may be used as dippers. A variety of chilled, crisp raw vegetables are a good choice — try carrot, cucumber or celery sticks, radishes, halved button mushrooms, cauliflower florets and green and red pepper rings. Arrange them on a serving dish, cover and chill for 1 hour.
Strips of pitta bread, toast fingers and breadsticks make more substantial dippers. Other possibilities are prawn and other small savoury crackers.

MICROWAVE MAGIC
To serve the dip warm, microwave at 100% (high) for 1 minute or until hot, then leave to stand for 1 minute. Stir well.
You can make the meatballs in advance, then reheat them: microwave at 100% (high) for 3-4 minutes or until hot, then leave to stand for 2 minutes.

PERFECT PARTNER FOR RICE & PASTA

MINCE IN A NEARLY ENDLESS VARIETY OF SAUCES MAKES AN IDEAL
ACCOMPANIMENT TO THESE INTERNATIONAL FAVOURITES

TURKEY & MUSHROOM RISOTTO

SERVES 4 · 25 MINUTES TO PREPARE · 1 HR TOTAL TIME
365 KCAL PER SERVING

25g/1oz sliced dried mushrooms
50g/2oz butter
2 garlic cloves, finely chopped
1 large onion, finely chopped
3 shallots, finely chopped
225g/½lb minced turkey
225g/½lb button mushrooms, finely sliced
150g/5oz wild rice, rinsed and drained
75g/3oz long grain white rice
1 tsp celery salt
125ml/4fl oz dry white wine
salt and freshly ground black pepper
1 tbls finely chopped fresh parsley
1 tbls finely chopped fresh chives

1 Put the dried mushrooms in a bowl with 125ml/4fl oz boiling water and leave to soak for 30 minutes.

2 Melt the butter in a large saucepan, add the garlic, onion and shallots and cook for 5 minutes, stirring constantly. Add the minced turkey and cook until the meat has lost its pinkness.

3 Add the sliced button mushrooms and cook for 5 minutes over low heat, stirring frequently. Stir in the wild rice and 575ml/1pt cold water, then bring to the boil. Cover the pan, reduce the heat and simmer for 40 minutes.

4 Add the long grain white rice with 150ml/5fl oz water, bring to the boil and cook for 10 minutes. Add the dried mushrooms to the pan together with their soaking liquid and the celery salt.

5 Add the white wine, then season to taste with salt and freshly ground black pepper and cook for 15 minutes over low heat.

6 Just before serving, fork in the parsley and chives. Remove the risotto from the heat and spoon it into a warm serving dish.

SWEDISH MEATBALLS

SERVES 6 · 40 MINS TO PREPARE
3/4 HR TOTAL TIME · 370 KCAL PER SERVING

75g/3oz dry breadcrumbs
175ml/6fl oz milk
75g/3oz butter
1 small onion, sliced
450g/1lb minced beef
125g/4oz minced pork
1 egg
1 tbls chopped fresh chives

1 tsp grated nutmeg
salt and pepper
fresh chives, to garnish

SAUCE
1 tbls flour
425ml/¾pt beef stock
3 tbls double cream

1 In a large bowl, soak the breadcrumbs in the milk until the milk is absorbed. Melt 25g/1oz butter in a frying-pan. Add the onion and fry over medium heat for 5 minutes or until soft. Leave to cool for a few minutes.

2 Transfer the onion to the breadcrumb mixture with a slotted spoon. Add the minced beef and pork, egg, chives, nutmeg, 2 teaspoons salt and pepper to taste and mix well. With your hands, roll the mixture into small balls.

3 Melt half the remaining butter in the frying pan and fry the meatballs, in batches, over medium-high heat for about 10 minutes. As each batch is cooked, remove to a dish lined with kitchen towels and place in a low oven.

4 To make the sauce, add the flour to the butter in the pan and cook for 2-3 minutes, stirring constantly. Stir in the stock and simmer for 5 minutes, stirring frequently, then add the cream and cook for 1 minute, stirring constantly. Pour the sauce over the meatballs and serve at once.

MEATBALL STROGANOFF

SERVES 6 · 40 MINS TO PREPARE
1 HR TOTAL TIME · 595 KCAL PER SERVING

700g/1½lb minced beef
50g/2oz fresh breadcrumbs
1 egg, beaten
4 tbls chopped parsley
2-4 tbls vegetable oil
1 onion, finely chopped

275g/10oz mushrooms, thinly sliced
50ml/2fl oz dry white wine
2 tsp Dijon mustard
275ml/½pt sour cream

1 Place the minced beef, breadcrumbs, egg, 2 tablespoons parsley and salt and pepper to taste into a bowl. Mix together thoroughly. Divide the mixture into 24 pieces and, with wet hands, roll each one into a ball.

2 Heat 2 tablespoons oil in a large frying-pan over medium heat. Fry the meatballs, in batches if necessary, for 10 minutes or until cooked through, turning frequently. As they cook, remove from the pan with a slotted spoon and drain on kitchen towels. Keep warm in a low oven.

3 Add the onion to the pan and cook for about 5 minutes or until golden, stirring frequently. Add the mushrooms and cook for a further 5 minutes, stirring occasionally, before adding the wine. Continue cooking over high heat for 5 minutes or until the liquid has reduced to just a few tablespoons, stirring constantly.

4 Stir the mustard into the sauce and return the meatballs to the pan for a further 2 minutes. Reduce the heat to low and stir in the cream. Cook for 1-2 minutes, stirring constantly, to heat the cream but don't allow the sauce to boil. Adjust the seasoning if necessary, then serve at once, sprinkled with the remaining chopped parsley.

TAGLIATELLE ALLA BOLOGNESE

SERVES 4 · 15 MINS TO PREPARE
1 HR 5 MINS TOTAL TIME · 580 KCAL PER SERVING

2 tbls olive oil
350g/12oz tagliatelle
Parmesan cheese, to serve
parsley sprigs, to garnish
SAUCE
25g/1oz butter
1 large onion, finely chopped

225g/½lb minced beef
¼ tsp dried mixed herbs
150ml/¼pt dry white wine
3 tbls tomato purée
salt and pepper

1 To make the Bolognese sauce, heat the butter and 1 tablespoon olive oil over medium heat in a large frying-pan. Add the onion and cook for 5 minutes until translucent, stirring occasionally. Add the minced beef to the pan and mix with the onions, using a wooden spoon to break up the mince. Continue cooking for a further 5 minutes or until the meat is brown, stirring constantly. Stir in the dried mixed herbs, wine, tomato purée and salt and pepper to taste, then simmer gently, uncovered, for 35 minutes.

2 Meanwhile, cook the pasta. Bring a large saucepan of salted water to the boil, add the remaining oil and then the pasta. Return to the boil and cook for 8-10 minutes or until *al dente*. To test the tagliatelle to see if it is ready, lift a piece out of the pan with a fork, leave to cool for a second or two, then bite into it. Carry on cooking for a minute or so if it's not yet done. Drain the pasta thoroughly. Divide between individual serving dishes and pour on the sauce. Shave some Parmesan over each portion, if liked, and serve immediately, garnished with parsley.

MEATBALLS WITH WALNUTS

SERVES 4-6 · 25 MINS TO PREPARE
1 HR 10 MINS TOTAL TIME · 640 KCAL PER SERVING.

700g/1½lb minced beef
2 tbls vegetable or walnut oil
125g/4oz shelled walnuts,
   chopped
125ml/4fl oz milk
2 slices wholemeal bread,
   crusts removed
1 egg, beaten
grated zest and juice of ½ lemon
salt and freshly ground black pepper
15g/½ oz margarine or butter
1 tbls plain flour
275ml/½pt beef stock
2 tbls double cream
walnut halves and lemon twists,
   to garnish

1 Heat the oil in a frying-pan, add the chopped walnuts and fry gently for 5 minutes, stirring often. Remove nuts from the pan with a slotted spoon and drain them well on kitchen towels. Reserve the cooking oil in the pan.

2 Transfer three-quarters of the nuts to a large bowl. Put the milk in a separate shallow bowl and add the bread. Press the bread down well with a fork to absorb the milk completely. Break up the soaked bread with the fork and add to the bowl with the nuts.

3 Add the minced beef, egg and lemon zest and juice and stir very thoroughly to mix. Season to taste with salt and pepper. Take heaped teaspoons of the mixture and, using floured hands, roll into about 24 balls.

4 Melt the margarine or butter in a large saucepan, sprinkle in the flour and stir over low heat for 1-2 minutes until straw-coloured. Gradually stir in the stock and simmer, stirring constantly, until thick and smooth.

5 Add the meatballs to the saucepan and bring to the boil. Lower the heat, cover and simmer the meatballs and sauce for 40 minutes.

6 Stir in the cream and remaining walnuts and heat thoroughly but gently. Taste and adjust the seasoning if necessary. Transfer to a warmed serving dish and serve at once straight from the dish.

COOK'S TIP
Walnut oil gives this dish a particularly good flavour. It is expensive if bought in this country, but if you are on holiday in France, it is worth buying a small bottle or can. Walnut oil can also be used in salad dressings to give a mild nutty flavour.

SERVING IDEAS
Serve with buttered ribbon noodles, garnished with walnut halves and lemon twists.

VARIATION
For a spicier sauce, add a pinch of cayenne.

SPAGHETTI WITH MEATBALLS

SERVES 4 · 30 MINS TO PREPARE
1 HR 10 MINS TOTAL TIME · 970 KCAL PER SERVING

SAUCE
25g/1oz butter
1 tbls olive oil
1 Spanish onion,
   finely chopped
1 garlic clove,
   finely chopped
125g/4oz
   mushrooms, sliced
400g/14oz tinned
   tomatoes
3 tbls tomato purée
1 bay leaf
1 small strip of lemon zest
salt and freshly ground
   black pepper
150ml/¼pt beef stock
1 tbls Worcestershire
   sauce

MEATBALLS
350g/12oz minced beef
350g/12oz minced pork
2 slices of bread, crusts
   removed, soaked in milk
2 garlic cloves, finely
   chopped
2 tbls fresh parsley
   finely chopped
salt and freshly ground
   black pepper
1 large egg, beaten
3 tbls flour
25g/1oz butter
2 tbls olive oil

350g/12oz spaghetti
freshly grated Parmesan
   cheese

1   To make the sauce: heat the butter and olive oil in a large heavy-based frying-pan. Sauté the finely chopped onion and garlic for 7-10 minutes or until soft, stirring occasionally. Add the mushrooms and sauté for a further 3-4 minutes or until lightly browned. Add the tinned tomatoes, tomato purée, bay leaf, lemon zest and beef stock. Season to taste, cover and simmer for 30 minutes, stirring occasionally.

2   Meanwhile make the meatballs: in a bowl combine the minced beef and pork, bread, and finely chopped garlic and parsley. Season to taste and stir in the egg to bind. Shape into 16 small meatballs. Sprinkle the flour onto a plate and lightly coat each of the meatballs in it, shaking off the excess.

3   Heat the butter and oil in a frying-pan large enough to take the meatballs in one layer. When the foaming has subsided, put in the meatballs and cook for 1-2 minutes on each side, or until evenly browned, turning them over with a spatula.

4   Stir the Worcestershire sauce into the tomato sauce and correct the seasoning. Transfer the meatballs to the tomato sauce, using a slotted spoon. Simmer for 20 minutes, turning the meatballs once.

5   Meanwhile, bring a large saucepan of salted water to the boil, add the spaghetti and cook for 15 minutes or until *al dente* - tender but still firm. Drain and rinse with very hot water. Arrange the spaghetti in a large heated serving dish. Spoon the meatballs and sauce on top. Serve with a bowl of freshly grated Parmesan cheese to sprinkle on top.

INGREDIENTS GUIDE
Parmesan cheese can be bought in a block or already grated. For the best taste, buy it whole and grate it yourself just before serving.

BAVARIAN MEATBALLS

THESE NOODLES ARE A SOUTH GERMAN
SPECIALITY CALLED SPAETZLE
SERVES 4 · 30 MINS TO PREPARE
1 HR TOTAL TIME · 850 KCAL PER SERVING

**450g/1lb lean
  minced beef**
**4 tbls fresh white
  breadcrumbs**
**½ tsp poultry
  seasoning**
1 tbls chopped parsley
**salt and freshly ground
  black pepper**
4 tbls milk
1 large egg, beaten
25g/1oz butter
1 tbls olive oil
**1 Spanish onion,
  finely chopped**
**125g/4oz mushrooms,
  finely chopped**

**275ml/½pt beef
  consommé**
150ml/¼pt sour cream

CARAWAY NOODLES
250g/9oz flour
**salt and freshly ground
  black pepper**
**2 large eggs,
  lightly beaten**
175ml/6fl oz milk
**2 tbls fresh white
  breadcrumbs**
1 tsp caraway seeds
4 tbls melted butter

1 In a bowl, combine the minced beef, breadcrumbs, poultry seasoning and finely chopped parsley. Season generously with salt and freshly ground black pepper to taste. Stir in the milk and beaten egg. With wet hands, shape the mixture into 24 balls.

2 Heat the butter and olive oil in a frying-pan. Brown the meatballs for 4 minutes, shaking the pan so they colour evenly. With a slotted spoon, transfer the meatballs to a plate and keep warm.

3 Sauté the onion and mushrooms in the pan for 5 minutes, or until beginning to soften, stirring occasionally with a wooden spoon.

4 Stir in the consommé and return the meatballs to the pan. Simmer, uncovered, for 25 minutes, or until the meatballs are cooked and the sauce has reduced by half.

5 Meanwhile, prepare the caraway noodles. Sift the flour with a pinch of salt into a bowl. Make a well in the centre and pour the beaten eggs and milk into it. With a wooden spoon, beat the eggs and milk, gradually incorporating the flour. Beat the batter until smooth. Bring a saucepan of salted water to the boil and press the batter with a wooden spoon through a wide-holed colander straight into the boiling water. Cook for 5 minutes, stirring occasionally. Drain and keep warm. In a saucepan, combine the breadcrumbs, caraway seeds and melted butter. Toss in the noodles until they are coated.

6 Transfer the meatballs to a heated serving dish. Stir the sour cream into the sauce and pour over the meatballs and scatter the noodles on top. Serve hot.

WHAT TO DRINK
Accompany this dish from the south of Germany with a glass of ice-cold lager.

PORK MEATBALLS

SERVES 4 · 20 MINS TO PREPARE
35 MINS TOTAL TIME · 360 KCAL PER SERVING

450g/1lb lean minced pork
4 tbls fresh white breadcrumbs
1 tsp dried sage
4 tbls milk
1 egg, beaten
50g/2 oz flour
olive oil, for frying

1 In a bowl, combine the minced pork, breadcrumbs and sage. Season generously with salt and pepper. Stir in the milk and beaten egg.

2 With wet hands to prevent the mixture from sticking to them, shape the mixture into 24 balls. Place the flour on a plate and coat each ball in flour before cooking.

3 Heat the butter and olive oil in a frying pan large enough to take them in one layer. Brown them on a high heat for 3-4 minutes, shaking the pan so that they colour as evenly as possible. Then reduce the heat and cook for a further 10 minutes until cooked through. With a slotted spoon, transfer the browned meatballs to a plate and keep warm until ready to serve..

SERVING SUGGESTIONS
Serve on a bed of tagliatelle with an accompaniment of fresh vegetables or a green salad.

PORK & VEAL MEATBALLS

SERVES 4 - 15 MINS TO PREPARE
30 MINS TOTAL TIME · 425 KCAL PER SERVING

MEATBALLS
225g/8oz minced pork
225g/8oz minced veal
1 small onion, grated
1 garlic clove, crushed
½ tsp dried thyme
½ tsp ground allspice
150g/5oz fresh white breadcrumbs
1 egg, beaten
4 tbls oil

SAUCE
15g/½oz butter
2 tbls plain flour
400g/14oz tin tomatoes
pinch of caster sugar
bouquet garni
GARNISH
3 tbls sour cream
10 black olives, stoned
lemon wedges
sprigs of parsley

1 Mix all the meatball ingredients together in a large bowl. Divide the mixture evenly into 20 balls, shaping them with wet hands. Heat the oil in a frying pan large enough to take the meatballs in one layer. Fry the meatballs over a high heat until no longer pink, then reduce the heat and cook for 10 minutes, turning frequently until cooked through. Transfer to a serving dish.

2 For the sauce, melt the butter in a small saucepan. Stir in the flour until well blended, then mix in the remaining ingredients. Bring slowly to the boil, stirring all the time, until thickened. Simmer sauce for 1-2 minutes. Season with salt and pepper to taste.

3 Sieve the sauce and pour over the meatballs in the dish. Drizzle sour cream over the top and garnish with the olives, lemon wedges and parsley.

CANNELLONI WITH MINCED BEEF FILLING

SERVES 6 · 30 MINS TO PREPARE
1³/4 HRS TOTAL TIME · 725 KCAL PER SERVING

700ml/1¼pt milk
125g/4oz butter
65g/2½ oz flour plus pinch of nutmeg
salt and freshly ground black pepper
50g/2oz fresh white breadcrumbs
50g/2oz Parmesan cheese, freshly grated
2 eggs
12 cannelloni tubes

FILLING
1 small carrot, very finely chopped
1 small onion, very finely chopped
1 celery stick, very finely chopped
25g/1oz butter
2 tbls vegetable oil
350g/12oz minced beef
100ml/3½fl oz red wine
1 tbls tomato purée dissolved in 125ml/4fl oz
    of meat stock, or in ½ stock cube dissolved in
    the same amount of water

1 To make the filling, put the carrot, onion, celery, butter and oil in a saucepan over low heat and sauté them gently for 10 minutes, stirring frequently. Add the meat, raise the heat to medium-high, and brown the meat well. Pour over the wine and boil the mixture briskly until the wine is nearly all evaporated.

2 Add the tomato purée and meat stock, bring to the boil and cook, covered, over very low heat for ½ hour or until the meat is done. Add a little more stock or warm water, if necessary, during cooking, but the juice should be quite thick.

3 To make the white sauce, bring the milk to simmering point and remove from the heat. Meanwhile, melt 75g/3oz butter in a heavy saucepan over very low heat. When melted, stir in the flour with a wooden spoon and cook for 1 minute until the mixture thickens. Remove the pan from the heat and add the hot milk a little at a time, stirring constantly, until the sauce is smooth. Season with nutmeg, salt and pepper, remove from the heat and reserve.

4 Ten minutes before the meat is ready, put the breadcrumbs and 2 tablespoons of the Parmesan in a bowl and pour over half of the meat cooking juices. Transfer the meat and the contents of the saucepan to a bowl, add the breadcrumbs and Parmesan mixture and the eggs and mix very thoroughly. Taste and adjust the seasoning. Heat the oven to 200°C/400°F/gas 6.

5 Butter a large shallow ovenproof dish. Spoon the meat mixture into the cannelloni tubes and lay them in the dish.

6 Spread the white sauce over the cannelloni tubes. Sprinkle over the rest of the Parmesan and dot with the rest of the butter. Bake for 15 minutes and serve at once.

INGREDIENTS GUIDE
Packets of cannelloni tubes which require no pre-cooking can be bought at large supermarkets.

LAMB & PASTA MEDLEY

SERVES 4 · 20 MINS TO PREPARE
55 MINS TOTAL TIME · 570 KCAL PER SERVING

2 tbls olive oil
1 onion, chopped
1 green pepper,
　deseeded and chopped
2 courgettes,
　finely chopped
450g/1lb minced lamb
400g/14oz tin tomatoes
275ml/½pt water
250g/9oz pasta shapes

½tsp dried basil
½tsp dried thyme
salt and freshly ground
　black pepper
125g/4oz mushrooms,
　sliced
grated Parmesan or
　Cheddar cheese to
　sprinkle (optional)

1 Heat the oil in a saucepan and fry the onion, green pepper and courgettes gently for 2-3 minutes until soft. Add the lamb, turn the heat to high and fry until the meat is evenly browned, stirring with a wooden spoon to remove any lumps. Pour off any excess fat.

2 Stir in the tomatoes with their juice and the water, breaking up the tomatoes with the spoon. Bring to the boil, stirring frequently.

3 Add the pasta, herbs and salt and pepper to taste and mix well. Cover the pan and simmer the lamb and pasta for 15 minutes. Stir in mushrooms and simmer uncovered, for 10 minutes. Serve the lamb and pasta medley at once with Parmesan or Cheddar cheese grated over the top if wished.

PASTA WITH SAUSAGE & COURGETTES

SERVES 4 · 10 MINS TO PREPARE
50 MINS TOTAL TIME · 650 KCAL PER SERVING

425ml/15fl oz bottle tomato sauce
1 tsp dried oregano
225g/½lb pasta shells
50g/2oz butter
2 tbls olive oil
225g/½lb minced beef
225g/½lb spicy Italian sausage, thinly sliced
2 medium-sized courgettes, thinly sliced

1 Bring a large saucepan of salted water to the boil, add 1 tablespoon olive oil and the pasta shells. Cook for 10-18 minutes or until *al dente*. Drain and keep warm.

2 Meanwhile, heat 15g/½oz butter and 1 tablespoon olive oil in a large frying pan. Add the beef and cook over a high heat, stirring constantly until lightly browned. Remove the meat from the pan with a slotted spoon and keep warm. Add 15g/½oz butter to the fat remaining in the pan and sauté the Italian sausage for 10 minutes. Add to the drained pasta shells with the cooked meat and keep warm.

3 Heat the tomato sauce and add the dried oregano. Keep warm. In a large frying-pan, heat the remaining butter and cook the courgettes until tender and lightly golden. Add to the pasta shells and mix well. Transfer the mixture to a large, heated serving platter, pour the tomato sauce over and serve immediately.

EASY CHILLI CON CARNE

THIS EVER-POPULAR MINCED
BEEF DISH IS PERFECT SERVED
WITH PLAIN BOILED RICE

SERVES 4 · 15 MINS TO PREPARE
1¼ HRS TOTAL TIME
515 KCAL PER SERVING

2 tbls vegetable oil
1 large onion, finely chopped
1 green pepper, deseeded
and chopped
1 red pepper, deseeded
and chopped
2 tsp hot chilli powder
2 tsp ground cumin
600g/1¼lb minced beef
2 tbls tomato purée
400g/14oz tin chopped
tomatoes
400g/14oz tin red kidney beans,
drained and rinsed
salt and freshly ground black
pepper
275ml/½pt sour cream
snipped fresh chives, to garnish

1 Heat the oil in a large frying-pan over medium heat. Add the onion and peppers and fry, stirring frequently, for 5 minutes or until softened but not browned. Stir in the chilli powder and cumin and continue to cook, stirring often, for 5 minutes.

2 Add the minced beef to the pan and mix with the other ingredients, using a spatula to break it up. Increase the heat to high and cook, stirring occasionally, for 5-8 minutes or until the meat is well browned. Spoon off any excess fat.

3 Add the tomato purée and stir until well blended. Stir in the tomatoes and the red kidney beans. Bring the mixture to the boil, then reduce the heat to low. Partially cover the pan with a lid and simmer for 30-40 minutes or until the meat and vegetables are cooked. Season with salt and pepper to taste. Pour the sour cream into a bowl and garnish with a sprinkling of chives; serve with the hot chilli.

WHAT TO DRINK
This strong-tasting dish needs a robust red wine such as a Navarra from Spain.

SERVING SUGGESTIONS
Chilli con Carne is an ideal dish for parties because it can be made a day ahead and reheated just before serving. Serve with a selection of toppings and let guests add their own, such as finely grated Cheddar cheese, plain Greek-style yogurt or finely diced avocado tossed with a little lemon juice. If you are feeding a large number of people on a tight budget, bulk out the meat with extra tinned beans and some frozen or tinned sweetcorn.

CURRIED MEATBALLS

SERVES 4 · 20 MINS TO PREPARE
40 MINS TOTAL TIME · 300 KCAL PER SERVING

450g/1lb minced beef
2 tbls tomato ketchup
2 tsp **Worcestershire**
  sauce
2 tsp English mustard
2 tsp mild curry powder
1 tsp salt

50g/2oz fresh
  white breadcrumbs
1 tbls vegetable oil
1 small onion,
  finely chopped
1 egg, beaten
vegetable oil, for frying

1 Put the minced beef, tomato ketchup, Worcestershire sauce, mustard, curry powder, salt and breadcrumbs in a bowl and stir well to mix.

2 Heat the oil in a saucepan, add the onion and fry for 5 minutes until soft and lightly coloured. Remove from the heat and stir into the minced beef mixture until well mixed in.

3 Add the beaten egg to bind the mixture together. Stir thoroughly. Taking one teaspoon of the prepared mixture at a time, roll it into about 30 small balls between floured hands.

4 Heat the oven to 110°C/225°F/gas ¼. Heat a little oil in a large frying-pan, add half the meatballs and fry gently for 8-10 minutes, turning occasionally, until golden brown and cooked through. Drain well on kitchen towels and keep hot in the oven while frying the remaining meatballs in the same way. Pile the meatballs on to a warmed serving dish and serve at once.

BITKIS

SERVES 4 · 15 MINS TO PREPARE
25 MINS TOTAL TIME · 440 KCAL PER SERVING.

350g/12oz minced beef
1 large onion, finely chopped
175g/6oz fresh breadcrumbs
3 tbls freshly chopped parsley
salt and freshly ground black pepper
225g/8oz tin tomatoes
150ml/¼pt sour cream
vegetable oil, for shallow frying
chopped fresh parsley, to garnish

1 In a bowl, mix together the beef, onion, half the breadcrumbs, the freshly chopped parsley and the salt and freshly ground black pepper to taste.

2 Divide the mixture into 12 and form each piece into a flat cake with your hands. Toss each cake in the remaining breadcrumbs to coat thoroughly and evenly.

3 Heat a little oil in a large frying-pan and shallow fry the bitkis for 5 minutes, turning once, until they are golden brown and crispy. Keep them warm over a very low heat while preparing the sauce.

4 Put the tomatoes and sour cream in a blender and work until smooth or rub the tomatoes through a sieve and beat in the cream. Season well, then pour the mixture into a saucepan and heat very gently until barely bubbling.

5 Arrange the bitkis on a bed of rice in a serving dish and pour the sauce over them. Garnish with parsley and serve with a fresh, crunchy cucumber, celery or green pepper salad.

SPICY TOMATO MEATBALLS

SERVES 6 · 10 MINS TO PREPARE
1½ HRS TOTAL TIME · 300 KCAL PER SERVING

4 tbls olive oil
2 onions, finely chopped
2 garlic cloves, crushed
450g/1lb tomatoes,
   skinned and chopped
2 tbls tomato purée
1 tsp sugar
1 tbls coriander seeds, crushed
freshly chopped parsley, to garnish

MEATBALLS
450g/1lb minced beef
250g/9oz minced pork
2.5cm/1in thick slice of white bread,
   crusts removed, soaked in cold water
   and squeezed dry
1 large egg, lightly beaten
½ tsp dried mint
salt and freshly ground black pepper

1 To make the sauce, heat 2 tablespoons oil in a saucepan. Fry the onion and garlic over medium heat for 10 minutes, until softened and lightly browned. Stir the tomatoes, tomato purée, sugar and coriander in with the onions and garlic. Cover the pan and simmer gently for 20-25 minutes, stirring occasionally.

2 To make the meatballs, mix together the beef, pork, bread, egg, mint and salt and pepper to taste. Using your hands, shape the mixture into about 24 balls.

3 Heat the remaining oil in a large, heavy-based frying-pan. Fry the meatballs for 5-8 minutes, turning frequently until browned all over. Pour off and discard any excess oil. Pour the sauce over, cover and simmer for 30 minutes, stirring occasionally. Adjust the seasoning. Spoon the meatballs and sauce into a warmed serving dish. Sprinkle with parsley and serve hot.

FREEZER FACTS
Freeze the cooked meatballs and sauce in a rigid container for up to 6 months. Defrost in the refrigerator overnight, then reheat gently in a saucepan for 30 minutes or until thoroughly heated through. If the sauce is too thick, add up to 150ml/¼pt water.

KOFTE WITH LEMON & CORIANDER SAUCE

GROUND LAMB FILLET IS GRILLED ON SKEWERS
TO MAKE THESE SUCCULENT KEBABS
SERVES 6 · 20 MINS TO PREPARE
30 MINS TOTAL TIME · 480 KCAL PER SERVING

900g/2lb lamb fillet, cubed
^{1}/2 tsp ground coriander
^{1}/2 tsp ground cumin
I garlic clove, crushed
I onion, roughly chopped
^{1}/2 tsp salt
handful of fresh chopped coriander
2 eggs, beaten

LEMON & CORIANDER SAUCE
4 egg yolks
4 tbls lemon juice
225ml/8fl oz water
25g/1oz fresh coriander leaves, chopped

1 Keeping the eggs aside, put all the remaining kofte ingredients in a food processor or blender and mix to a smooth paste. Remove the paste from the blender and gradually mix in the beaten eggs. Knead the mixture with your hands until it forms a pliable dough.

2 Dampen your hands so that the meat mixture does not stick to them, then break off egg-sized portions and slip two portions on to each skewer

3 Mould each portion of meat paste along the skewer to form a sausage shape. Heat the grill, and oil the grill pan. Place the kebabs in the grill pan and cook for 10 minutes under high heat until well browned, turning the skewers frequently.

4 Meanwhile, make the sauce. Whisk the egg yolks in a heatproof bowl until pale and fluffy. Whisk in the lemon juice and water. Place the bowl over a saucepan of gently simmering water and stir until it thickens. Stir in the coriander leaves and serve immediately with the kofte.

SERVING IDEAS

Lay the kebabs on a bed of rice or serve Greek-style in warmed pitta breads with shredded lettuce. Add a sprinkling of coriander leaves and don't forget the lemon wedges — their flavour helps to bring out the taste.

SERVING SUGGESTIONS
This recipe makes about 40 meatballs which, when served with other dishes as part of a Greek meze, would be enough for at least 10 people. As a main course, served with rice and a salad, this recipe would serve about 6.

WHAT TO DRINK
Red wine is best with these delicious herby meatballs. If you don't want to drink the Cypriot wine Othello, you might like to try a young Chianti or Beaujolais, or a Côtes du Rhône.

GREEK LAMB MEATBALLS

IDEAL AS A BUFFET DISH, SERVED HOT OR COLD, THESE BITE-SIZED SAVOURIES – KNOWN AS KEFTETHES IN GREECE – ALSO MAKE A TASTY SUPPER DISH

SERVES 6 · 35 MINS TO PREPARE · 1 HR 35 MINS TOTAL TIME WITH STANDING · 400 KCAL PER SERVING

50ml/2fl oz milk
125g/4oz fresh white breadcrumbs
700g/1½lb minced lamb
1 onion, finely chopped
3-4 tbls chopped fresh parsley
1 tsp chopped fresh mint, or ½tsp dried
1 tbls mature cheddar cheese, grated (optional)
2 eggs, beaten
salt and freshly ground black pepper
50g/2oz flour
olive oil, for frying
mint leaves, to garnish

1 Mix the milk and breadcrumbs in a bowl. Then, using your fingers, squeeze the milk from the breadcrumbs and pour it away.

2 Add the lamb, onion, herbs, cheese, if using, and eggs to the bowl and mix well. Season to taste, cover and leave to stand for 30 minutes.

3 Break off a portion about the size of a walnut and roll it into a ball between the palms of your hands. Continue to make meatballs in this way until you have used up all the mince. Sprinkle the flour on a plate, season and roll each meatball in it until evenly coated.

4 Pour the olive oil into a large frying pan to a depth of 12mm/½in and heat until very hot. Fry the meatballs, in batches if necessary, turning frequently until evenly browned.

5 As the meatballs cook, remove them from the pan with a slotted spoon and drain on kitchen towels. If serving hot, keep warm in a low oven; if serving cold, leave to cool then transfer to the fridge until ready to serve. Garnish with mint leaves to serve.

MINCED VEAL PATTIES

SERVES 4 · 25 MINS TO PREPARE · 2¾HRS TOTAL TIME WITH CHILLING · 550 KCAL PER SERVING

400g/14oz minced veal	175g/6oz mushrooms,
salt and pepper	sliced
275ml/½pt double cream	150ml/¼pt dry white wine
flour, for dusting	15g/½ oz butter
50g/2oz butter	15g/½ oz flour

1 Season the meat generously and mix with half the cream. Purée in a blender or food processor until smooth.

2 Sprinkle a work surface with flour. Divide the veal purée into eight portions and form each into a small patty about 1cm/½in thick. Chill for 2 hours.

3 Heat 25g/1oz butter in a small pan and fry the mushrooms until just soft. Melt the remaining butter in a large frying-pan. When the foam subsides, add the patties and fry for 4-5 minutes or until golden brown on both sides. Lift out, drain on kitchen towels and keep warm.

4 Add the wine to the frying-pan and scrape up all the crusty bits from the bottom and sides. Pour in the remaining cream and stir in the mushrooms. Mix together over low heat.

5 Mash the butter to a smooth paste with the flour. Add it to the pan a little at a time, stirring well. When it has all been added, heat the sauce gently for 2-3 minutes. Pour over the patties to serve.

MINCED BEEF WITH CHICORY & ORANGE

SERVES 4 · 20 MINS TO PREPARE · 30 MINS TOTAL TIME 385 KCAL PER SERVING

3 medium-sized oranges
15g/½oz butter
700g/1½ lb minced beef
1 garlic clove, finely chopped
4 small heads of white chicory, thinly sliced
½ tbls freshly chopped parsley
½ tbls freshly chopped thyme
8 green olives, stoned and quartered
GARNISH
chicory leaves, orange slices and fresh parsley

1 Cut the rind and pith from two of the oranges. Cut the flesh into quarters and thinly slice it. Squeeze the juice from the remaining orange.

2 Melt the butter in a large, heavy-based frying-pan over a high heat. Add the minced beef and break it up. Add the garlic and cook, stirring, until the beef browns, about 5-7 minutes.

3 Lower the heat and mix in the chicory and herbs. Add the orange juice and cook gently, uncovered, for 5 minutes, stirring.

4 Stir in the sliced oranges and the olives. Cook for one minute, garnish with the chicory leaves, orange slices and parsley and serve at once.

VEAL KHEEMA WITH MINT

SERVES 4 · 20 MINUTES TO PREPARE
1 HR 20 MINS TOTAL TIME · 160 KCAL PER SERVING

450g/1lb minced veal
1 tbls oil
2 onions, finely chopped
2 cm/¾in fresh root ginger, peeled and finely chopped
2 garlic cloves, finely chopped
½ fresh green chilli, deseeded and finely chopped
½ tsp allspice
½ tsp turmeric
6 tomatoes, skinned, deseeded and chopped
3 tbls fresh mint, chopped
2 tbls lemon juice
1 tsp garam masala
salt
sprigs of fresh mint, to garnish

1 Place the minced veal in a sieve and rinse under cold running water, then press with the back of a spoon to remove all excess water.

2 Heat the oil in a heavy-based saucepan and fry the onions and ginger for 4-5 minutes, until golden.

3 Add the meat and fry until browned. Drain off any excess fat, then add the garlic, chilli, allspice and turmeric. Mix well and cook for 1-2 minutes, stirring constantly, over medium heat.

4 Stir in the tomatoes, mint, lemon juice, garam masala and 275ml/½pt water. Bring to the boil, stirring frequently, then lower the heat and cook, uncovered, for 30-40 minutes, stirring occasionally, until the meat is cooked through and the sauce has thickened. Season to taste with salt.

5 Transfer to a heated serving dish and garnish with sprigs of mint.

BEEF KHEEMA WITH PEAS

KHEEMA IS THE INDIAN WORD FOR MINCED MEAT

SERVES 4 · 20 MINUTES TO PREPARE · 1½HRS TOTAL TIME
430 KCAL PER SERVING

3 tbls oil
2 onions, finely chopped
1 green chilli, deseeded
  and finely chopped
1.5cm/½in fresh root
  ginger, peeled and
  finely chopped
1 tsp turmeric
450g/1lb minced beef
150ml/¼pt plain
  yogurt

½ tsp salt
4 hard-boiled eggs,
  shelled
125g/4oz frozen peas,
  defrosted
2 tomatoes, skinned
  and quartered

GARNISH
1 tsp garam masala
2 tbls chopped coriander

1 Heat the oil in a large, heavy-based saucepan. Add the onions and fry over medium heat for 5-6 minutes, stirring frequently, until golden brown.

2 Add the chilli, ginger and turmeric and cook for a further 1-2 minutes, stirring frequently, then add the meat, increase the heat and cook for 1-2 minutes, until the meat is browned.

3 Stir in the yogurt, salt and 275ml/½pt water. Bring to the boil, then lower the heat and simmer gently for 30-40 minutes. Add the eggs, peas and tomatoes, cover and simmer for 15 minutes. Transfer to a heated serving dish and sprinkle with garam masala and coriander. Serve at once.

COOK'S TIP
When adding the yogurt, add only a spoonful at a time, stirring constantly. Make sure you incorporate each spoonful well before adding the next.

FREEZER FACTS
Root ginger can be very suc cessfully stored in the freezer. Simply keep it in a plastic bag. It can be peeled and cut almost as soon as you take it out of the freezer.

QUICK BEEF CURRY

SERVES 4 · 15 MINS TO PRPEPARE · 30 MINS TOTAL TIME
· 400 KCAL PER SERVING

450g/1lb lean minced beef
1 large onion, chopped
1 garlic clove, crushed
1 tbls curry powder
¼ tsp ground ginger
¼ tsp ground cumin
1 dessert apple, peeled
  and grated
2 tbls sultanas
  or seedless raisins
275g/10oz tin condensed
  beef consommé
salt and freshly ground
  black pepper
125g/4oz mushrooms, quartered

1 Place the beef, onion and garlic in a heavy-based saucepan and fry over medium heat until the beef is well browned, stirring constantly to break up any lumps.

2 Stir in the spices and cook for 2 minutes, then stir in the apple, sultanas and the beef consommé. Season with salt and pepper to taste. Bring to the boil, then simmer gently for 5 minutes.

3 Stir in the mushrooms and simmer for a further 10 minutes. Taste and adjust seasoning. Serve at once with boiled rice and sliced onions.

INGREDIENTS GUIDE

Curry powder is made from many different spices, including allspice, cardamom, chilli, cumin, saffron and turmeric. It is available in various strengths, from mild to very hot, so be sure to check the label carefully and use a hot one sparingly.

COUNTRY RISOTTO

SERVES 4 · 20 MINS TO PREPARE · 1 HR TOTAL TIME
· 435 KCAL PER SERVING

1 tbls vegetable oil
1 large onion, finely chopped
1 garlic clove, crushed
125g/4oz mushrooms, quartered or halved
  depending on size
50g/2oz cooked ham, diced
250g/9oz minced beef
200g/7oz medium- or long-grain rice,
  preferably Italian
400g/14oz tin tomatoes
400ml/14fl oz hot chicken stock
¼ tsp dried thyme
¼ tsp dried oregano
salt and freshly ground black pepper
25g/1oz Parmesan cheese, grated

1 Heat the oil in a large heavy-based saucepan and gently cook the onion until soft and translucent. Stir in the garlic, mushrooms and ham. Add the minced meat and cook until brown, stirring all the time.

2 Add the rice to the meat mixture and stir well. Add the tomatoes with their juice, half the hot stock and the dried herbs.

3 Season with salt and pepper to taste and stir well, breaking up the tomatoes against the side of the pan.

4 Bring to the boil, then lower the heat, cover the pan and simmer for 40 minutes or until the rice is tender. Check the contents of the pan frequently and add more hot stock as it is absorbed. The texture of the risotto should be fairly creamy – neither too dry nor too liquid. Serve hot, sprinkled with the grated Parmesan cheese.

SERVING IDEAS
Serve with a crisp and crunchy green salad.

COOK'S TIPS
Italian rice is best for risotto because is is less likely to break up than other types of rice which have a tendency to go mushy.
Different types of rice absorb different quantities of liquid, but the stock should always be added hot and in small amounts. Stop adding liquid when the rice is *al dente* (tender but still with a little 'bite' to each grain) and there is just enough liquid to bubble gently. A risotto should never be dry.

MEXICAN MINCE

SERVES 4 · 30 MINS TO PREPARE · 1¼ HRS TOTAL TIME
555 KCAL PER SERVING

450g/1lb minced beef
1-2 tbls vegetable oil
1 small onion,
   finely chopped
3-4 tsp chilli powder
2 tbls quick-cooking
   porridge oats
1¼ cups beef stock
1 tbls tomato paste
pinch of freshly
   grated nutmeg

salt and freshly ground
   black pepper
375g/13oz packet of
   frozen sweetcorn with
   sweet peppers
1 large or 2 medium
   avocados
1 tbls lemon juice
125g/4oz Cheddar
   cheese, cut into
   2.5cm/1in cubes

1 Heat 1 tablespoon oil in a heavy-based saucepan. Add the beef and fry over moderate heat for 3 minutes, stirring constantly until all the beef has browned, breaking up any lumps with a wooden spoon. Remove the beef with a slotted spoon. Add the onion to the pan and fry for 5 minutes until soft and lightly coloured, adding a further tablespoon of oil if necessary, to prevent overbrowning.

2 Return the beef to the pan, stir in 3 teaspoons chilli powder, then the oats, stock, tomato paste, nutmeg, salt to taste and a light sprinkling of pepper. Bring to the boil, stirring, then reduce the heat, cover and simmer gently for 40-45 minutes or until the oats are soft and the meat cooked.

3 Stir the drained sweetcorn and peppers into the beef mixture and continue to cook, uncovered, for 5 minutes until most of the excess liquid has evaporated. Taste and adjust seasoning, adding more chilli if a slightly hotter flavour is preferred.

4 Just before serving, cut the avocado in half lengthways and discard the stone. Cut into quarters lengthways and peel away the skin, then cut the flesh into neat thin slices lengthways. Brush with the lemon juice to prevent the avocado discolouring.

5 Stir the cheese into the beef until just beginning to melt, then spoon the mixture into a warmed serving dish and arrange the avocado slices around the edge. Serve at once.

SERVING SUGGESTIONS

The minced beef, cheese and avocado make this dish quite heavy. To counteract this, serve with plain, boiled rice and a crisp green salad.

VARIATION

If you do not have any chilli powder (available in jars from supermarkets), use the same quantity of mild curry powder; this will season the beef, but will not be sufficient to give a strong curry flavour.

MEXICAN BEEF LAYER

SERVES 4 · 35 MINS TO PREPARE · 1 HR 10 MINS TOTAL TIME
600 KCAL PER SERVING

1 tbls vegetable oil

2 onions, finely chopped

4 streaky bacon rashers, finely chopped

250g/9oz minced beef

1 garlic clove, crushed

1 bay leaf

2 tsp tomato purée

1 tbls tomato ketchup

1 tbls sultanas

1 tbls Demerara sugar

½ tsp chilli powder

150ml/¼pt beef stock

salt and freshly ground black pepper

175g/6oz Italian risotto rice

1 green pepper, deseeded and finely chopped

425g/15oz tin red kidney beans, drained

margarine, for greasing

1 small avocado, to garnish

275ml/½pt thick home-made tomato sauce,
   to serve

1 Heat the oil in a large heavy-based saucepan, add the chopped onion and the chopped bacon and fry gently for 5 minutes, until the onion is soft and lightly coloured. With a slotted spoon, transfer the onion and bacon to a plate and set aside until later.

2 Add the minced beef to the saucepan, and fry it over a brisk heat for a few minutes, until the meat is browned all over. Stir it with a wooden spoon to break up any lumps.

3 Return the onion and bacon to the pan with the garlic, the bay leaf, tomato purée, tomato ketchup, sultanas, sugar, chilli powder and stock. Cover the pan, bring almost to the boil then lower heat and cook very gently for about 30 minutes, stirring occasionally.

4 Meanwhile, bring a large saucepan of salted water to the boil, add the rice and cook for 10 minutes, then add the green pepper and cook for a further 5 minutes or until the rice is tender. Drain.

5 Remove the meat mixture from the heat. Liberally grease a 1L/2pt pudding basin. Spoon a layer of rice into the basin, followed by a layer of meat mixture, then a layer of beans. Repeat these layers once more, then top with a final layer of rice. Cover the basin with foil and place in a large saucepan. Pour in boiling water to come halfway up the sides of the basin, cover and simmer the beef layer for 40 minutes.

6 Remove the pudding basin from the saucepan, using oven gloves. Cool slightly, remove the foil and run a knife around the basin. Insert a warmed serving plate on top and carefully turn out the beef layer. Peel and slice the avocado. Top the beef layer with avocado slices and serve at once with tomato sauce.

HOT FROM THE OVEN

MOUTH-WATERING BAKES WITH CRISPY TOPPINGS ARE IDEAL FOR FAMILY SUPPERS. COMBINING MEAT, VEGETABLES AND EITHER POTATO, RICE OR PASTA IN ONE HANDY DISH MAKES THEM EASY AND DELICIOUS

TRADITIONAL SHEPHERD'S PIE

THIS TRADITIONAL DISH OF MINCED LAMB
AND MASHED POTATO IS A FIRM FAVOURITE
WITH ALL THE FAMILY

SERVES 4 · 45 MINS TO PREPARE
1¼ HRS TOTAL TIME · 530 KCAL PER SERVING

1 tbls vegetable oil
1 onion, chopped
700g/1½lb minced lamb
1 tbls tomato purée
1 tsp Worcestershire sauce
1 tbls flour
150ml/¼pt lamb stock
1 tsp freshly grated nutmeg
1 tsp chopped fresh rosemary
salt and freshly ground black pepper

TOPPING
700g/1½lb potatoes, cut into even-sized pieces
25g/1oz butter
150ml/¼pt milk

1 Heat the oil in a large frying pan over medium heat, add the onion and fry for 5 minutes or until softened and translucent, stirring often. Add the mince and cook for 10 minutes or until it loses its pink colour, breaking it up with a wooden spoon.

2 Turn the heat to low and carefully pour off the fat. Add the tomato purée and Worcestershire sauce and sprinkle on the flour, stirring. Pour in the stock and stir well. Add the nutmeg and rosemary and season with salt and pepper to taste. Cook for a further 10 minutes, stirring occasionally.

3 Meanwhile, heat the oven to 180°C/350°F/gas 4. Put the potatoes into a large pan of salted water and bring to the boil. Cover and simmer for 20 minutes or until the potatoes are tender when tested with a fork. Drain the potatoes and return to the pan. Add the butter and milk and season with salt and pepper to taste. Mash until soft and creamy.

4 Put the mince mixture into a 1.1L/2pt ovenproof dish and pile the mashed potato on top. Roughen up with a fork. Cook on the top shelf of the oven for 30 minutes or until golden brown. Serve hot.

MINCE & POTATO HASH WITH POACHED EGGS

SERVES 6 · 30 MINS TO PREPARE
45 MINS TOTAL TIME · 345 KCAL PER SERVING

350g/12oz potatoes, scrubbed
25g/1oz butter
1 tbls olive oil
2 green peppers deseeded and diced
1 Spanish onion, chopped
700g/1½lb minced beef
400g/14oz tin tomatoes
6 tbls fresh parsley, chopped
2 tbls Worcestershire sauce
4 tbls white wine vinegar
6 large eggs

1 Boil the potatoes in salted water for 15 minutes or until tender. Drain, cool, then peel off the skin and dice the potatoes. In a large frying pan heat the butter and olive oil. Add the onion and peppers and cook over medium heat for 5 minutes, stirring occasionally.

2 Add the beef to the onion and peppers and cook gently until the meat loses its pinkness. Add the tinned tomatoes, cover and simmer for 20 minutes until cooked. Add the potatoes, parsley and Worcestershire sauce. Season to taste. Keep hot.

3 Poach the eggs: fill a saucepan with water, add the vinegar, bring to the boil and reduce the heat to a simmer. One at a time, break the eggs into a cup and slip them into the water. Simmer gently for 3-4 minutes. Remove with a slotted spoon. Turn out the meat mixture onto a large heated serving platter. Arrange the poached eggs on top. Garnish with sprigs of parsley and serve at once.

MOUSSAKA

SERVES 6 · 1 HR TO PREPARE
2 HRS TOTAL TIME WITH PRECOOKING AND DRAINING
800 KCAL PER SERVING

900g/2lb aubergines,
   cut into 1cm/¹/₂in slices
225ml/8fl oz sunflower oil
450g/1lb onions, sliced
2 garlic cloves, sliced
450g/1lb minced lamb
700g/1¹/₂lb tomatoes,
   skinned and sliced
2 tbls beef stock
¹/₂ tsp dried basil
ground black pepper

250g/9oz Gruyère or
   Cheddar cheese, sliced
2 tbls chopped parsley

TOPPING
15g/¹/₂oz butter
15g/¹/₂oz plain flour
275ml/¹/₂pt milk
2 eggs, separated
pinch of freshly
   grated nutmeg

1 Put the sliced aubergines in a colander and sprinkle with salt. Set the colander on a plate and leave to drain for 30 minutes.

2 Heat about 50ml/2fl oz oil in a large, heavy-based frying pan. Add the onions and garlic and fry over medium heat, stirring occasionally for about 15 minutes, until golden. Remove from the pan with a slotted spoon, drain on kitchen towels and set aside.

3 Heat a further 25ml/1fl oz oil in the pan. Add the minced lamb and fry gently, stirring often to remove any lumps, for 5-10 minutes until the meat has lost its pinkness. Remove the mince from the pan with a slotted spoon, drain on kitchen towels and set aside with the onions.

4 Rinse the aubergines under cold running water and pat dry with kitchen towels. Add a further 50ml/2fl oz oil to the pan, add the aubergines and fry over medium heat, turning occasionally, for 10-15 minutes until golden on both sides. Add more oil as necessary. Drain the fried aubergines thoroughly on kitchen towels.

5 Meanwhile, put the tomatoes in a saucepan, add the beef stock and basil and season with salt and pepper to taste. Cook this over a gentle heat for 10-15 minutes, stirring occasionally with a wooden spoon, to make a thick, pulpy sauce.

6 Heat the oven to 180°C/350°F/gas 4. Brush a 30 x 20 x 5cm/12 x 8 x 2in baking dish with oil. Make layers of aubergines, cheese, minced lamb and onions, seasoning the layers with salt and pepper and moistening with the tomato sauce. Repeat until all the ingredients are used.

7 Make the topping: melt the butter in a saucepan, sprinkle in the flour and stir over low heat until straw-coloured. Remove from the heat and gradually stir in the milk. Return to the heat and simmer, stirring, until thickened and smooth. Remove from heat and allow to cool slightly. Beat in the egg yolks and a pinch of nutmeg. Whisk the egg whites until soft peaks form, then fold lightly into the sauce.

8 Pour the topping over the dish and bake in the oven for about 1 hour, until the topping is browned. Remove from oven and sprinkle with the parsley. Serve hot, straight from the dish.

VARIATIONS

In Greece, natural yogurt is often used to thicken the topping mixture, or it may be flavoured with Greek cheese, such as shredded Haloumi. In this case, omit the cheese from the layers.

WATCHPOINTS

Aubergines soak up oil like blotting paper, so have extra ready to add to the pan if it shows signs of becoming dry.
Draining the fried aubergines on kitchen towels is essential, otherwise the finished dish will be too oily.

GREEK MACARONI PIE

SERVES 6
3/4 HR TO PREPARE
2 1/4 HRS TOTAL TIME
700 KCAL PER SERVING

1 onion, chopped
1 garlic clove, crushed
2 tbls olive oil
700g/1 1/2lb minced beef
salt and freshly ground black pepper
1/2 tsp ground cinnamon
1/2 tbls dried oregano
225g/1/2lb passata (crushed, strained tomatoes)
50g/2oz butter, plus extra for greasing
50g/2oz flour
425ml/3/4pt milk
1/4 tsp nutmeg
50g/2oz freshly grated Parmesan cheese
225g/1/2lb small macaroni
1 egg, lightly beaten
200g/7oz Cheddar cheese, coarsely grated

1 Heat the oven to 190°C/375°F/gas 5. Sauté the onion and garlic in the oil in a large, deep-sided pan until soft. Add the beef and salt and pepper to taste. Cook, stirring, until the meat loses its pink colour. Pour off and discard the fat and stir in the cinnamon, oregano and passata. Put the mixture to one side.

2 To make the white sauce, melt 40g/1 1/2oz butter in a large saucepan and stir in the flour. Pour in the milk gradually, stirring constantly, and cook, stirring, until thickened. Add salt and pepper to taste, the nutmeg and the Parmesan cheese.

3 Meanwhile, cook the macaroni in a large saucepan of boiling salted water for 15-20 minutes or until just tender. Drain well and return to the pan. Pour in the egg and the remaining butter, mixing it in well with a wooden spoon.

4 Grease a shallow 1.7L/3pt baking dish. Make layers of half the macaroni, all the meat, half the Cheddar, then the remaining macaroni. Whisk the white sauce, then pour over the top, shaking the dish gently so that the sauce settles. Sprinkle on the remaining Cheddar.

5 Bake the pie in the oven for 1 hour or until it is golden brown and bubbling, then serve hot.

INGREDIENTS GUIDE
Passata is usually sold in cartons; you can buy it from delicatessens and some supermarkets. If you can't find it, use 400g/14oz tinned tomatoes, blended until smooth.

SHEPHERD'S SOUFFLÉ

SERVES 4 · 30 MINS TO PREPARE
1¼ HRS TOTAL TIME · 525 KCAL PER SERVING

450g/1lb potatoes
3 tbls vegetable oil
1 onion, chopped
100g/4oz mushrooms,
  sliced
1 green pepper,
  deseeded and chopped

450g/1lb minced beef
1 tbls plain flour
225g/8oz tin tomatoes
1 tsp dried mixed herbs
3 eggs, separated
2 tbls milk
25g/1oz butter

1 Heat the oven to 190°C/375°F/gas 5. Bring the potatoes to the boil in salted water, lower the heat and cook for 20 minutes or until tender.

2 Meanwhile, heat the oil in a heavy-based saucepan, add the onion, mushrooms and pepper and fry over medium heat for 5 minutes until the onion is soft and translucent. Add the minced beef, turn the heat to high and fry until the meat is evenly browned. Sprinkle in the flour and stir over low heat for 1-2 minutes. Add the tomatoes with their juice, the herbs and salt and pepper to taste. Turn the minced beef mixture into a 1.4L/2½pt soufflé dish.

3 In a clean, dry bowl whisk the egg whites until they are standing in stiff peaks. Drain the potatoes. Mash them thoroughly, and beat in the milk, butter and the egg yolks. Season with salt and pepper to taste, then lightly fold in the egg whites.

4 Spoon the potato mixture over the mince and bake in the oven for 45 minutes until well risen and golden brown. Serve the soufflé at once, while risen.

BEEF & CELERY CRISP

SERVES 4 · 30 MINS TO PREPARE
1 HR TOTAL TIME · 595 KCAL PER SERVING

15g/½oz margarine
1 tbls vegetable oil
4 celery sticks, chopped
700g/1½lb minced beef
100g/4oz mushrooms,
  sliced
1 tbls mushroom ketchup

275g/10oz tin condensed
  celery soup
BATTER
100g/4oz plain flour
2 eggs
150ml/¼pt milk
3 tbls water

1 Heat the oven to 200°C/400°F/gas 6. Grease an ovenproof casserole dish. Heat the margarine and oil in a large heavy-based saucepan, add the celery and cook gently until it is softened but not browned.

2 Add the minced beef to the pan and cook until the meat is evenly browned. Stir in the mushrooms and cook for a further 1-2 minutes. Add the mushroom ketchup and celery soup. Stir well until the mixture is simmering. Continue to cook over low heat for 5-10 minutes. Season to taste and turn into the greased casserole.

3 Make the batter: sift the flour with a pinch of salt into a large bowl and make a well in the centre. Beat the eggs with the milk and water and gradually add to the bowl working the flour into the centre. Beat the mixture well until it becomes a smooth batter. Carefully spoon the batter on top of the beef, then cook for 25-30 minutes, until the batter is well risen and brown on top. Serve at once, straight from the dish.

BEEF & MUSHROOM CHARLOTTE

SERVES 4-6
1 HR TO PREPARE
1 1/2 HRS TOTAL TIME
675 KCAL PER SERVING

700g/1 1/2lb minced beef
1 tbls vegetable oil
1 large onion, chopped
4 tbls fresh white
breadcrumbs
275ml/1/2pt beef stock
2 tbls tomato purée
1 tbls Worcestershire
sauce
1 tbls English mustard
salt and freshly ground
black pepper
2 tbls plain flour
8 slices wholemeal
bread, crusts removed
40g/1 1/2oz margarine
250g/9oz mushrooms,
chopped
25g/1oz Cheddar cheese

1 Heat the oil in a large heavy-based saucepan, add the minced beef and onion and cook over medium to high heat for about 3-4 minutes, stirring until the beef has lost its pinkness.

2 Stir in the breadcrumbs, stock, tomato purée, Worcestershire sauce, mustard and salt and pepper to taste. Bring to the boil, stirring, then lower the heat, cover the pan and simmer gently for 30 minutes, or until the meat is cooked. Blend the flour with 2 tablespoons of water, stir into the pan and stir constantly over low heat until thickened.

3 Heat the oven to 190°C/375°F/gas 5. Spread margarine on the slices of bread and cut each slice into three strips. Lightly grease a 1.7L/3pt casserole or soufflé dish. Use 12 of the bread strips, buttered side down, to line the base and sides of the dish.

4 Scatter half the mushrooms over the bread strips. Pour in the beef mixture, then scatter the remaining mushrooms over the surface. Arrange the remaining bread fingers, buttered side up, over the top, sprinkle with the grated cheese. Bake the Charlotte in the oven for 30 minutes until crisp and golden brown on top. Serve at once, straight from the dish.

VARIATION
Instead of the mushrooms, use the same amount of finely grated carrot in the Charlotte.

PREPARATION
This dish can be prepared in advance to the end of stage 2, then assembled when you are ready to cook and eat it.

CRUSTY-TOPPED BEEF

SERVES 4 · 25 MINS TO PREPARE
1 HR 10 MINS TOTAL TIME· 465 KCAL PER SERVING

1 tbls oil
1 onion, finely chopped
1 garlic clove, crushed
450g/1lb minced beef
2 tbls plain flour
300ml/¹/₂pt beef stock
1 bouquet garni
2 tsp tomato purée
1 tbls sherry
salt and freshly ground black pepper
125g/4oz mushrooms, thinly sliced
125g/4oz chicken livers, chopped

TOPPING
2 long crusty rolls
50g/2oz butter with herbs and garlic

1 Heat the oil in a heavy-based frying pan and add the onion and garlic. Cook until soft, then add the mince and stir well to break up any lumps. Cook over medium heat until browned, stirring frequently.

2 Add the remaining ingredients except for the livers and topping ingredients, cover and cook for 15 minutes. Add the livers and cook for a further 15 minutes. Transfer to a casserole dish and remove the bouquet garni.

3 Cut the rolls into 1.5cm/¹/₂in diagonal slices and toast one side. Spread the other side with herb and garlic butter and arrange the slices, slightly over-lapping, on top of the casserole. Brown evenly under a hot grill. Serve at once.

INGREDIENTS GUIDE

Look out for flavoured butters in the shops or make your own herb and garlic butter, by creaming 50g/2oz butter with 1tbls dried herbs and 1 crushed garlic clove.

BEEF & SPINACH SAVOURY

SERVES 4 · 45 MINS TO PREPARE
1¼ HRS TOTAL TIME · 635 KCAL PER SERVING

450g/1lb minced beef
15g/½oz butter
1 tbls vegetable oil
1 large onion, chopped
225g/8oz tin tomatoes, chopped
1 tbls tomato purée
1 tbls mushroom ketchup
salt and freshly ground black pepper
100g/4oz vermicelli
2 x 275g/10oz packets frozen chopped spinach
1 large egg
1 tbls grated Parmesan cheese
½ tsp freshly grated nutmeg
150ml/¼pt sour cream
100g/4oz mushrooms, sliced
2 large tomatoes, sliced
100g/4oz Cheddar cheese, grated
margarine, for greasing

1 Heat the butter and oil in a large saucepan, add the onion and fry gently for 5 minutes, until soft and lightly coloured. Add the mince, turn the heat to high and fry for a further 5 minutes or until the meat has lost all its pinkness, stirring with a wooden spoon.

2 Add the tomatoes with their juice, tomato purée and mushroom ketchup. Stir well, bring to the boil and season with salt and pepper to taste. Lower the heat, cover and simmer for about 30 minutes.

3 Meanwhile, bring a large saucepan of salted water to the boil, add the vermicelli and cook for about 5 minutes, until just tender. Cook the chopped spinach according to the instructions on the packet.

4 Heat the oven to 180°C/350°F/gas 4. Grease a shallow ovenproof dish.

5 Drain the vermicelli and cut it up roughly. Beat the egg and Parmesan cheese together in a bowl, and season with pepper and nutmeg. Add the chopped vermicelli and fork it through well. Spoon over base of dish.

6 Drain the spinach and put it into a bowl. Stir in the sour cream.

7 Spoon the beef and tomato mixture over the vermicelli. Arrange the sliced mushrooms on top and evenly spoon over the spinach and cream mixture.

8 Top with the tomato slices and sprinkle with the grated cheese. Cook in the oven for 20-30 minutes, until the cheese topping is melted and golden.

INGREDIENTS GUIDE
Vermicelli, very thin pasta, is sold in coiled bundles, rather like birds' nests, and is available in packets from supermarkets. It cooks in half the time taken for spaghetti.

BEEF & COURGETTE LAYER

SERVES 6 · 45 MINS TO PREPARE
1¼ HRS TOTAL TIME · 345 KCAL PER SERVING

1 tbls vegetable oil
2 large onions, finely chopped
450g/1lb minced beef
2 celery sticks, thinly sliced
2 carrots, thinly sliced
2 tbls plain flour
2 tsp tomato purée
150ml/¼pt beef stock
salt and freshly ground black pepper
450g/1lb courgettes, thinly sliced lengthways
450g/1lb tomatoes, skinned and thickly sliced

CHEESE SAUCE
25g/1oz butter
2 tbls plain flour
275ml/½pt milk
50g/2oz mature Cheddar cheese, grated
2tbls grated Parmesan cheese

1 Heat the oil in a heavy based frying pan, then add the onions and cook for 3-4 minutes. Add the minced beef and continue cooking until the meat has lost its pinkness.

2 Add the celery sticks, carrots and flour and blend well. Add the beef stock and tomato purée and bring to the boil, stirring constantly. Season to taste. Continue cooking gently for 20-25 minutes until the meat is cooked.

3 Bring a saucepan of water to boiling point, add the courgettes and boil for 5 minutes. Drain the courgettes and set aside. Heat the oven to 190°/375°/gas 5.

4 To make the sauce: melt the butter, add the flour, stirring constantly over low heat for 3 minutes, then increase the heat to medium and gradually add the milk, whisking constantly until the sauce thickens and boils. Then simmer over a very low heat for 3-4 minutes, stirring frequently. Stir in the cheeses and season with salt and pepper to taste.

5 Spread half of the mince mixture over the base of a large, shallow casserole, cover with half of the tomatoes and courgettes, then repeat the layers. Spoon the cheese sauce over the top and put in the oven for 30 minutes until cooked and brown on top.

SAUSAGE & POTATO CASSEROLE

SERVES 4
3/4 HR TO PREPARE
1³/4 HRS TOTAL TIME
580 KCAL PER SERVING

450g/1lb minced pork
25g/1oz margarine or
   butter
2 large onions, thinly
   sliced
3 celery sticks, chopped
700g/1½lb potatoes,
   peeled
1 egg, beaten
50g/2oz dry parsley and
   thyme stuffing
2 tbls vegetable oil
225g/8oz tin tomatoes
salt and freshly ground
   black pepper

1 Melt the margarine in a large frying pan, add the onions and celery and cook over moderate heat for 10-15 minutes until softened but not coloured. With a slotted spoon, remove the vegetables from the pan and place them in a layer in the bottom of a 2L/3½pt casserole with a lid.

2 Put the potatoes into a large saucepan and cover with cold water. Cover the pan and bring to the boil. Lower the heat and simmer the potatoes for 5 minutes. Drain the potatoes thoroughly and set aside until cool enough to handle.

3 Meanwhile put the minced pork in a mixing bowl, season with salt and pepper to taste and add beaten egg to bind the mixture together. Mix thoroughly. Take spoonfuls of the prepared mixture and roll into about 12 small sausages. Roll the sausages in the dry stuffing mix, coating them thoroughly.

4 Heat the oven to 190°C/375°F/gas 5. Pour the oil into the remaining fat in the frying pan, add the sausages and fry for about 10 minutes, turning until lightly browned on all sides.

5 While the sausages are cooking, cut the potatoes into 5mm/¼in slices. Arrange the browned sausages over the cooked vegetable mixture in the casserole. Pour the tomatoes and their juice over the sausages. Arrange the potato slices overlapping on top and cover the casserole. Cook in the oven for 1 hour and serve hot.

VARIATIONS
Use 125g/4oz mushrooms, sliced, instead of the celery, and replace the tomatoes with a small tin of cream of mushroom soup.

SERVING SUGGESTIONS
To brown the top of the casserole, heat the grill to high, and brush melted margarine over the potatoes. Place under the grill.

CREAMY MINCE & COURGETTES

LAYERS OF MINCED BEEF, MUSHROOMS,
COURGETTES AND A CREAMY SAUCE
MAKE THIS A DELICIOUS
SAVOURY DISH
SERVES 6 · 10 MINS TO PREPARE
1¹/₂ HRS TOTAL TIME · 675 KCAL PER SERVING

2 tbls olive oil
1 onion, chopped
1 garlic clove, crushed
700g/1½lb lean minced beef
1 tbls tomato purée
1 beef stock cube
1 tsp cornflour
salt and freshly ground black pepper
225g/½lb button mushrooms, sliced
2 tsp fresh rosemary, chopped
450g/1lb courgettes
200ml/7fl oz crème fraîche

1 Heat the oven to 200°C/400°F/gas 6. Heat 1 tablespoon oil in a heavy-based frying pan and add the onion and garlic. Cook until soft, then add the mince and stir well to break up any lumps. Cook over medium heat until browned, stirring frequently.

2 Add the tomato purée, crumbled stock cube and cornflour to the pan, stir well and cook for a further 5 minutes. Adjust seasoning to taste. Spoon half the mince mixture into a 1.4L/2½pt ovenproof dish and spread flat. Set aside the rest in a cool place.

3 Add the remaining oil to the frying pan and heat through. Add the mushrooms and cook over high heat, stirring regularly, until browned. Spoon the mushrooms over the mince layer in the ovenproof dish. Sprinkle the rosemary over the mushrooms.

4 Slice the courgettes diagonally. Put them in the frying pan and cook over low heat until just transparent. Layer half the courgette slices over the mushrooms.

5 Spread 3 tablespoons of the crème fraîche over the layer of courgettes, then spoon the remaining mince mixture on top and smooth the surface. Layer the remaining courgettes on top of the mince. Top with the remaining crème fraîche. Bake in the oven for 35 minutes.

VARIATIONS
To make a larger version for a party, double all the ingredients and bake for 1¼ hours. Cover with foil towards the end of the cooking time.

SERVING SUGGESTIONS
Serve with green beans, sliced carrots and creamy mashed potatoes. For a summer dish, serve the minced beef layer with a fresh green salad and warm slices of pitta bread.

CRISPY MINCED BEEF

SERVES 4 · 25 MINS TO PREPARE
1 HR 10 MINS TOTAL TIME · 490 KCAL PER SERVING

I tbls vegetable oil
3 onions, sliced
450g/1lb minced beef
2 tbls plain flour
2 tsp mustard powder
400g/14oz tin tomatoes
150ml/¼pt beef stock

25g/1oz seedless raisins

TOPPING
2 small packets
plain potato crisps
50g/2oz Cheddar
cheese, grated

1 Heat the oil in a large frying pan with a lid, add the onions and fry gently for 10 minutes, stirring occasionally, until browned. Add the minced beef and fry, for 5-10 minutes until the beef has lost all its pinkness. Remove from the heat.

2 In a bowl, mix the flour and mustard powder to a smooth paste with a little of the tomato juice from the tin. Stir in the tomatoes with the remaining juice from the tin and the beef stock.

3 Add the tomato mixture to the pan and return to the heat. Bring to the boil, stirring constantly. Continue to cook for 1-3 minutes, and stir until the mixture thickens. Lower the heat and season with salt and pepper to taste. Stir in raisins, cover and simmer for a further 20 minutes.

4 Heat the grill to high. Spoon the mince mixture into a large shallow ovenproof dish. Sprinkle the crisps over the surface, then spread the grated cheese on top.

5 Grill for 2-3 minutes until the cheese is melted and bubbling and the topping is golden brown. Serve at once, straight from the dish.

MINCED BEEF COBBLER

SERVES 4 · 15 MINS TO PREPARE
1¼ HRS TOTAL TIME
595 KCAL PER SERVING

2 tbls vegetable oil
2 red peppers, sliced
I onion, chopped
I tsp chilli powder
450g/1lb minced beef
400g/14oz tin tomatoes
I beef stock cube

SCONES
225g/½lb wholemeal
flour
2 tsp baking powder
50g/2oz butter
150ml/¼pt milk

1 Heat the oil in a large saucepan over medium heat, add the peppers and onion and fry for 5 minutes or until softened, stirring now and then. Add the chilli powder and cook for a further 2 minutes, stirring constantly.

2 Add the mince and mix with the other ingredients, using a spatula to break it up. Add the tomatoes and crumble in the stock cube. Stir and leave to simmer for 30 minutes, stirring occasionally.

3 Heat the oven to 200°C/400°F/gas 6. To make the scones, sift the flour and baking powder into a bowl and rub in the butter. Set aside one tablespoon milk and stir the rest into the flour to form a soft dough. Lightly dust your work surface with flour and roll the dough out 12mm/½in thick. Cut out 12-14 circles with a diameter of 5cm/2in each.

4 Put the mince into a 1.1L/2pt ovenproof dish and overlap the scones evenly around the edge. Brush the scones with the remaining milk and bake in the oven for 20-25 minutes until the scones are golden brown. Serve at once.

PIZZA PORK BAKE

SERVES 6 · 20 MINS TO PREPARE · 50 MINS TOTAL TIME · 660 KCAL PER SERVING

450g/1lb minced pork
2 tbls vegetable oil
1 large onion, chopped
1 garlic clove, crushed
1 medium red pepper,
  deseeded and chopped
100g/4 oz mushrooms,
  sliced
275ml/¹/₂pt bottle
  tomato sauce
¹/₂ tsp Italian seasoning
salt and freshly ground
  black pepper
225g/8oz Cheddar
  cheese, grated
25g/1oz Parmesan
  cheese, grated

BATTER
100g/4oz plain flour
¹/₂ tsp salt
2 eggs
175ml/6fl oz milk
1tbls vegetable oil
¹/₂ tsp Italian seasoning

1 Heat the oven to 200°C/400°F/gas 6. Heat 2 tablespoons oil in a frying pan and gently fry the pork until it has lost its pinkness. Add the onion, garlic, red pepper and mushrooms and cook gently until the vegetables are soft.

2 Pour off any fat from the pan, then stir in the tomato sauce and Italian seasoning. Season to taste with salt and freshly ground black pepper. Put the pork mixture into a 2L/3¹/₂pt shallow ovenproof dish. Scatter the Cheddar cheese over the top.

3 To make the batter, sift the flour and salt into a bowl and make a well in the centre. Beat the eggs with the milk and pour into the well. With a wooden spoon, gradually draw the flour into the liquid until it is all incorporated. Stir in the oil and Italian seasoning. Beat well until the mixture forms a smooth batter.

4 Pour the batter over the cheese-topped pork mixture. Be sure to press the pork mixture firmly into the baking dish, otherwise the batter will seep down into it rather than forming a golden brown crust on top. Sprinkle over the Parmesan cheese. Bake in the oven for 25-30 minutes or until the topping is set and golden brown.

5 Invert the dish over a large warmed serving plate so that the batter crust is on the bottom, like a pizza. Cut into squares to serve. If you are in a hurry, simply serve the pork bake straight from the dish with the batter on top like a pie crust.

TRADITIONAL LASAGNA

SERVES 4 · 30 MINS TO PREPARE
2 HRS TOTAL TIME· 840 KCAL PER SERVING

50g/2oz butter
1 tbls olive oil
1 onion, chopped
4 unsmoked streaky bacon rashers, cut into strips
450g/1lb minced beef
225g/½lb chicken livers, roughly chopped
400g/14oz tin tomatoes
150ml/¼pt dry red wine
2 tbls tomato purée
½ tsp dried basil
½ tsp grated nutmeg
salt and freshly ground black pepper
50g/2oz flour
575ml/1pt milk
100g/4oz 'no need to precook' lasagna
100g/4oz mozzarella, grated

1 Heat half the butter and the oil in a large saucepan or sauté pan over medium heat. Add the onion and fry for 5 minutes or until soft, stirring often. Add the bacon and cook for 2-3 minutes or until the bacon is just cooked.

2 Add the mince and use a wooden spoon or spatula to break it up. Cook for 3-5 minutes or until browned, stirring constantly. Add the livers and cook for a further 2-3 minutes or until the liver is no longer pink, stirring frequently.

3 Stir in the tomatoes, wine, tomato purée, dried basil, half the grated nutmeg and salt and pepper to taste. Reduce the heat to low and simmer, covered, for 30 minutes, stirring occasionally.

4 Remove the lid and increase the heat to medium. Continue to cook for a further 20-30 minutes or until reduced and thickened.

5 Heat the oven to 220°C/425°F/gas 7. Melt the remaining butter in a small saucepan over low heat and add the flour. Cook for 3 minutes, stirring constantly. Increase the heat to medium and gradually add the milk, stirring constantly, until the sauce boils and thickens. Add the remaining nutmeg and salt to taste and simmer over very low heat for 3 minutes, stirring often.

6 Pour half of the meat sauce into a 1.1L/2pt gratin dish and arrange a layer of lasagna on top. Pour just under half of the white sauce over the lasagna. Cover this with the remaining meat sauce and another layer of lasagna. Pour on the remaining white sauce and sprinkle the grated cheese over the top. Bake for 30-40 minutes or until the cheese is golden brown and bubbling and the pasta is cooked, covering the dish with foil if necessary. Serve at once.

WHAT TO DRINK

Try a Montepulciano d'Abruzzo, a full-bodied red wine from Italy, with this substantial and richly flavoured dish.

1. Heat the oven to 180°C/350°F/gas 4. Melt the margarine in a frying-pan, add the onion and apple and fry gently for about 5 minutes until soft and lightly coloured.

2. Stir the curry powder into the pan with the onion and apple and cook, stirring, for 2 minutes. Stir in the apricot jam and cook, stirring, for one further minute.

3. Put the bread in a large bowl and moisten it with 2-3 tablespoons of the milk. Break it up with a fork and add the minced lamb, curried onion and apple mixture, raisins and lemon juice. Stir everything together well and season with salt and pepper to taste.

4. Transfer the meat mixture to a shallow ovenproof dish and pat it down, smoothing the surface.

5. In a bowl, beat the remaining milk with the eggs and season with salt and pepper to taste. Pour the egg mixture on to the mince mixture in the dish.

6. Stick the bay leaves into the top of the mixture and scatter the almonds over the surface. Cook in the oven for 45 minutes or until the custard is set and golden.

7. Serve hot, straight from the dish, with fluffy boiled white rice and traditional curry accompaniments such as sliced onion, cucumber and tomato, desiccated coconut, chutney and poppadoms.

SOUTH AFRICAN BOBOTIE

SERVES 4 · 30 MINS TO PREPARE
1¼ HRS TOTAL TIME · 550 KCAL PER SERVING

700g/1½lb cooked lamb, all visible fat removed, minced
15g/½oz margarine or butter
1 onion, finely chopped
1 dessert apple, peeled, cored and chopped
1 tbls mild curry powder
1 tbls apricot jam, sieved
1 thick slice white bread, crusts removed
275ml/½pt milk
25g/1oz seeded raisins
squeeze of lemon juice
salt and freshly ground black pepper
2 eggs, beaten
2 bay leaves
25g/1oz flaked almonds

COOK'S TIP
Be careful not to overcook the dish: the custard can quickly become leathery and the meat mixture dry if it is overcooked.

MACARONI & MINCED BEEF BAKE

SERVES 4 · 10 MINS TO PREPARE
1½ HRS TOTAL TIME · 615 KCAL PER SERVING

2 tbls corn oil
1 onion, peeled and finely chopped
1 tbls cumin seeds
¼ tsp chilli powder
450g/1lb minced beef
400g/14oz tin of chopped Italian tomatoes
450ml/¾pt beef stock
1 large tin sweetcorn
175g/6oz short macaroni or pasta twirls
75g/3oz Cheddar cheese, grated

1 Heat the oven to 180°C/350°F/gas 4. Heat the oil in a large, heatproof casserole dish on the hob. Add the onion and cook gently over medium heat until soft.

2 Add the cumin seeds and chilli powder and cook for a further 30 seconds. Add the mince and cook until browned, stirring constantly.

3 Pour in the tomatoes and stock, then stir in the sweetcorn, including any liquid. Add the pasta and stir. Bake in the heated oven, uncovered, for 50 minutes.

4 Fifteen minutes before the end of the cooking time, remove the dish from the oven, stir the pasta and mince together, sprinkle the grated cheese over the top and return to the oven. Continue cooking to the end of the cooking time. Serve at once.

HACHIS PARMENTIER

SERVES 4 · 30 MINS TO PREPARE
1¼ HRS TOTAL TIME · 700 KCAL PER SERVING

65g/2½oz butter
1 Spanish onion, sliced
4 tomatoes, blanched, skinned and diced
450g/1lb minced beef
1 tbls tomato purée
salt and freshly ground black pepper

50g/2oz Gruyère cheese, grated

POTATO PURÉE
900g/2lb floury potatoes
150ml/¼pt hot milk
50g/2oz butter

1 Heat the oven to 230°C/450°F/gas 8. Heat 40g/ 1½oz butter in a heavy-based saucepan, add the onion and sauté for 7-10 minutes until soft. Add the tomatoes and continue to cook for a further 5 minutes. Stir in the minced beef and tomato purée. Season to taste and simmer for 10 minutes, stirring occasionally. Keep warm.

2 To make the potato purée, cook the potatoes in boiling salted water for 20 minutes until tender but not mushy; drain well. Mash them through a sieve. Beat in the hot milk and finally add the butter in small pieces. Season to taste.

3 Butter a 1.7L/3pt baking dish and cover the base with half the potato purée. Spread the meat mixture over it and cover with the remaining potato purée. Sprinkle with the grated cheese and dot with the remaining butter. Bake for 15-20 minutes until the top is golden brown.

BAKED EGGS MEXICANA

SERVES 4 · 40 MINS TO PREPARE
1¼ HRS TOTAL TIME · 290 KCAL PER SERVING

2 tbls olive oil
1 onion, chopped
2 garlic cloves, crushed
225g/¹/₂lb minced beef
400g/14oz tin chopped tomatoes
¹/₂ red pepper, de-seeded and diced
2 courgettes, grated
1 tbls tomato purée
¹/₂ tsp chilli powder
hot pepper sauce
4 eggs
large pinch of paprika
sprig of parsley to garnish

1 Heat the oven to 180°C/350°F/gas 4. Heat the oil in a heavy-based saucepan over medium heat and add the onion and garlic. Fry for 5 minutes until soft and translucent. Add the minced beef. Continue to cook until the meat has lost its pinkness.

2 Stir in the tomatoes, red pepper, courgettes, tomato purée, chilli powder and a dash of hot pepper sauce and stir well. Continue cooking for 20 minutes until the meat is cooked. Spoon into a shallow ovenproof dish.

3 Make a dent in one quarter of the mixture with a spoon and carefully break an egg into it, then repeat with the other three quarters.

4 .Place in the oven and bake for 10 minutes or until the eggs are just set. Sprinkle with the paprika and garnish with a sprig of parsley, if wished. Serve at once.

MEATLOAVES

FROM A HUMBLE MEATLOAF FOR A SIMPLE SUPPER
TO A MOCK BEEF WELLINGTON IDEAL FOR A PARTY,
THERE IS A MEATLOAF FOR EVERY OCCASION

TURKEY & CHESTNUT PLAIT

MAKES 2 PLAITS, EACH ONE SERVES 4
45 MINS TO PREPARE · 2 HRS TOTAL TIME PLUS COOLING
630 KCAL PER SERVING

175g/6oz brown rice
2 vegetable stock cubes
50g/2oz butter
2 celery sticks, sliced
450g/1lb leeks, sliced
450g/1lb minced turkey
225g/½lb button mushrooms, halved
225g/8oz tin unsweetened chestnut purée
240g/8½oz tinned unsweetened chestnuts, drained
1 tbls vegetable oil
½ onion, chopped
275ml/½pt red wine
3 tbls cranberry sauce
1 tsp dried thyme
2 x 250g/9oz packs puff pastry
1 egg yolk, lightly beaten

1 Put the rice and one stock cube in 400ml/14fl oz water. Bring to the boil, lower the heat, cover and simmer for 35-40 minutes. Allow to cool.

2 Melt the butter. Add the celery, leeks and minced turkey. Stir over low heat for 20 minutes. Stir in the mushrooms and 3 tablespoons chestnut purée. Leave to cool, then add the rice and chestnuts.

3 Heat the oven to 200°C/400°F/gas 6. To make the gravy, heat the oil in a saucepan and add the onion. Stir over medium heat for 5 minutes. Add the remaining chestnut purée and 1 tablespoon red wine. Mix into a paste. Add the rest of the wine, 275ml/½pt water, the remaining stock cube, cranberry sauce and thyme. Boil, then simmer for 30 minutes.

4 Meanwhile, roll out each piece of pastry to roughly 30 x 30cm/12 x 12in. Spoon half the turkey mixture along the centre of each one. Make an equal number of diagonal cuts 25mm/1in apart along the uncovered pastry at each side to within 12mm/½in of the filling.

5 Brush the cut sides with water. Take one strip and fold it over the filling. Take one from the other side and fold it across. Repeat to make a plait. Brush each plait with egg yolk and place on a baking sheet. Bake for 30 minutes or until golden. Strain the gravy and pour into a warmed sauceboat, then serve at once, with the plaits.

MIDWEST MEATLOAF

SERVES 6 · 30 MINS TO PREPARE
1 HR TOTAL TIME. · 425 KCAL PER SERVING

3 tbls olive oil
2 garlic cloves, crushed
1 large onion, chopped
1 red pepper, deseeded and diced
1 yellow pepper, deseeded and diced
900g/2lb minced beef
3 slices of white bread, soaked in water
2 tbls stuffed green olives, thinly sliced
3 tbls tomato ketchup
2 tbls fresh tarragon, chopped
2 tbls fresh chives, chopped
2 tbls fresh parsley, chopped
1 egg, beaten
225g/8oz streaky bacon, with rinds removed
tomatoes, quartered, to garnish

1 Heat the oven to 180°C/350°F/gas 4. Heat the oil in a large, heavy-based frying pan. Add the garlic and onion and cook over moderate heat for 5 minutes. Stir in the peppers and cook for a further 5 minutes.

2 Transfer the mixture to a large serving bowl. Add the soaked bread after squeezing it dry, minced beef, olives, tomato ketchup, herbs, salt and pepper and beaten egg, then use your fingertips to mix until all the ingredients are well combined.

3 Put the mixture in a roasting tin or ovenproof serving dish. Shape into a loaf. Using the bacon rashers, make a lattice-work pattern on top of the meatloaf, then place in the centre of the oven and bake for one hour. When it is cooked, remove the meatloaf from the oven and leave to cool for about 5 minutes before serving. Garnish with fresh tomato quarters.

MEATLOAF STROGANOFF

SERVES 4 ·30 MINS TO PREPARE
1½ HRS TOTAL TIME · 570 KCAL PER SERVING

1 tbls vegetable oil	½ tsp mustard powder
250g/9oz leeks, chopped	2 eggs, beaten
350g/12oz mushrooms, chopped	salt and freshly ground black pepper
1 tbls sour cream	margarine for greasing
450g/1lb minced beef	parsley sprigs, sliced
450g/1lb minced veal	mushrooms and
75g/3oz fresh white breadcrumbs	mushroom ketchup, to garnish

1 Heat the oven to 180°C/350°F/gas 4. Grease 1kg/2lb loaf tin, lining the base with greaseproof paper. Heat the oil and fry the leeks until soft. Remove and set aside. Fry half the mushrooms until tender. Stir in the sour cream, then remove from heat.

2 Combine the meats in a bowl. Add the leeks, bread-crumbs and mustard, then slowly stir in the eggs. Season to taste and stir well. Spoon half the meat mixture into the loaf tin and press down. Make a groove about 2.cm/1in wide down the centre of the meat. Fill this with fried mushrooms, then cover with the remaining meat.

3 Place the tin on a baking sheet, cover with foil and cook for 1 hour. Remove from the oven and leave to stand for 10 minutes. Press the surface of the loaf to drain any surplus liquid. Run a knife around the sides of the tin, Place an inverted serving plate on top and turn out the loaf. Garnish with mushroom slices, ketchup and parsley sprigs. Serve at once.

FRUIT & NUT MEAT ROLL

SERVES 6 · 30 MINS TO PREPARE
1½ HRS TOTAL TIME ·455 KCAL PER SERVING

	STUFFING
450g/1lb minced beef	50g/2oz fresh white breadcrumbs
250g/9oz minced pork	50g/2oz prunes, soaked, stoned and chopped
2 bunches spring onions, very finely chopped	2 celery sticks, chopped
1 large egg, beaten	1 dessert apple, peeled and grated
salt and freshly ground black pepper	50g/2oz shelled walnuts, finely chopped
150ml/¼pt beef stock	2 tbls dry sherry
	1 tsp dried mixed herbs

1 Heat the oven to 180°C/350°F/gas 4. In a bowl, mix the meats and spring onions. Add the egg, salt and pepper, mix thoroughly. Refrigerate.

2 To make the stuffing, mix all the ingredients. Season with salt and pepper to taste. Spread the meat mix-ture smoothly on to a sheet of greaseproof paper 37.5 × 30cm/ 15 × 12in. Place another sheet on top, and with a rolling pin, shape the meat to the paper size. Trim the edges.

3 Remove the top sheet of paper. Spoon the stuffing on to a short edge of the meat. Roll the meat like a Swiss roll over the stuffing. Keep the roll on the paper and place it in a shallow baking tin. Ease the paper out. Pour the stock over the roll and bake for about 1 hour until firm, basting frequently. Serve hot.

MELTING BEEF ROLL

SERVES 6 · 10 MINS TO PREPARE
1 HR TOTAL TIME · 595 KCAL PER SERVING

700g/1½lb minced beef
50g/2oz fresh white breadcrumbs
2 eggs, beaten
1 tsp dried oregano
1 garlic clove, crushed
salt and freshly ground black pepper
225g/8oz mozzarella cheese, sliced
vegetable oil, for greasing
tomato slices, to garnish

1 Heat the oven to 190°C/375°F/gas 5. Put the beef, breadcrumbs, eggs, oregano and garlic into a bowl. Season to taste and mix thoroughly.

2 Brush a sheet of foil about 45 x 30cm/18 x 12in with oil. Place the beef mixture in the centre. Pat into a 28 x 20cm/11 x 8in rectangle.

3 Arrange about three-quarters of the cheese slices on the beef, leaving a border of about 2.5cm/1in all round. Starting at one short end, roll up the beef like a Swiss roll. Press the join to seal well and press together the ends of the roll to seal in the cheese. Turn the beef so that the join is underneath. Lift the roll on its foil, and place in a roasting tin. Bake in the oven for about 45 minutes until browned.

4 Lift the meat on to an ovenproof serving dish. Arrange the remaining cheese slices on top, then return to the oven until the cheese has melted. Serve at once, cut into slices and garnished with tomatoes.

MOCK ROAST WITH ONION SAUCE

SERVES 4 · 15 MINS TO PREPARE
1 HR 5 MINS TOTAL TIME · 480 KCAL PER SERVING

700g/1½lb minced beef
450g/1lb onions
1 slice bread, crusts removed and crumbled
1 egg, beaten
salt and freshly ground black pepper
2 tbls vegetable oil
1 tbls brown sugar
75ml/3fl oz beef stock

1 Heat the oven to 180°C/350°F/gas 4. Grate 1 onion and slice the rest. Mix the minced beef in a bowl with the grated onion, breadcrumbs, egg and salt and pepper to taste. Turn the mixture into a small roasting dish. With your hands, form it into a flat, not thick, loaf shape. Keep the surface smooth. Cook, uncovered, for 25 minutes.

2 Meanwhile, heat the oil in a heavy-based saucepan, add the sliced onions and cook over a gentle heat until they are soft. Stir in the sugar, then the beef stock. Cook for 5 minutes. Remove the loaf from the oven and drain off the fat. Spoon the sauce over the loaf, return to the oven and cook for 25 minutes. Serve hot, cut into slices.

STUFFED MEATLOAF

THIS POPULAR MEATLOAF, POLPETTONO ALL
SICILIANA, IS SOMETIMES ROLLED IN A
WHOLE THIN SLICE OF BEEF OR VEAL.
HOWEVER, IT IS MUCH EASIER
TO WRAP IT IN FOIL
SERVES 6 · 40 MINS TO PREPARE
2 HOURS TOTAL TIME · 450 KCAL PER SERVING

1 slice white bread
  without crusts
900g/2lb minced beef
1 garlic clove
1 medium-sized onion,
  finely chopped
2 tbls parsley, finely
  chopped
salt and freshly ground
  black pepper
4 large eggs, beaten
olive oil for greasing

STUFFING
2 hard-boiled eggs,
  chopped
50g/2oz salami, skinned
  and cut into small strips
50g/2oz Provolone or
  Cacciocavalle cheese
  cut into small dice

SAUCE
1 tbls olive oil
1 onion, finely chopped
1 tbls tomato purée
225ml/8fl oz strong red wine

1 Moisten the slice of bread with a little water, then squeeze it dry and crumble it over the meat. Crush the garlic clove in a garlic press and scatter it over the bread and meat. Add the finely chopped onion and the parsley. Season to taste and stir thoroughly. Mix in the beaten egg.

2 Grease a large double sheet of thick foil with a little olive oil and pat out the meat mixture into a flat square layer on the foil. It should be about 15mm/¹/₂in thick.

3 Pile the hard-boiled eggs, salami and cheese dice in the centre of the meat layer. Lift two opposite edges of the foil and fold the uncovered sides of the meat layer over the stuffing. Pat it into a neat roll enclosing the stuffing. Fold the foil over the roll, enclosing it completely. Fold up the ends to make a neat parcel.

4 To make the sauce, heat the olive oil in a heavy ovenproof casserole. Fry the onion in the oil until soft. Add the foil-wrapped meat.

5 Mix the tomato purée with the wine, then pour into the casserole. Add 50ml/2fl oz water. As soon as the liquid bubbles, reduce the heat to very low and cover the casserole securely. Simmer the meat roll for 1¹/₂ hours. Top up the sauce with a little boiling water if it appears to be drying out.

6 Turn off the heat. Remove the roll parcel from the casserole. Undo the foil, and tip the meat roll onto a warmed platter. To serve hot, pour the sauce over the roll and serve at once.

7 To eat the meatloaf cold, cover the roll loosely with the foil and leave to cool. Cool the sauce and strain off any excess fat, then serve the roll cold, with the cold sauce handed round separately in a jug.

CARROT MEAT ROLL

SERVES 4 - 6 · 3/4 HR TO PREPARE
2 HRS TOTAL TIME · 570 KCAL PER SERVING

700g/1½lb lean minced beef
1 large slice bread, crusts removed
2 eggs, beaten
1 onion, finely grated
salt and freshly ground black pepper
3 tbls tomato ketchup
4 tsp soft light brown sugar
350g/12oz carrots, finely grated
50g/2oz fresh breadcrumbs
4 tbls parsley, chopped
cauliflower florets, stuffed green
  olives and fresh parsley, to garnish

1 Heat the oven to 180°C/350°F/gas 4. Cut out a piece of foil about 44 × 42cm/18 × 16in.

2 Put the bread in a shallow dish and pour over a little water. Allow to soak, then squeeze out the water. Crumble the bread into the beef in a bowl. Add half the beaten eggs, together with the onion and salt and pepper to taste. Mix well.

3 Turn the meat mixture on to the centre of the foil and pat it out to make a firm rectangle about 33 × 25 × 1cm/13 × 10x ½in.

4 Mix the ketchup with the brown sugar in a bowl and brush half the mixture over the meat.

5 In another bowl, mix the grated carrots with the breadcrumbs, parsley, the remaining egg, and season with salt and pepper to taste. Spread the mixture over the meat and, with your hands, pat it down evenly.

6 Starting from a short edge, roll up the meat like a Swiss roll. Smooth any cracks in the meat as you roll it up. Slide the roll to the centre of the foil and seal the two short edges of foil together leaving space around the roll. Seal the ends of the foil.

7 Lift into a roasting tin. Bake in the oven for 1 hour. Fold back the foil and brush the roll with the remaining ketchup mixture. Return to the oven, uncovered, on a high shelf, for 15 minutes. Using two fish slices, carefully transfer the meat roll to a warmed serving dish. Garnish with cauliflower, olives and parsley.

WATCHPOINT

It is important to pack the meat mixture firmly when making the rectangle shape on the foil otherwise there will be a lot of cracks on the outside surface and the meat roll will fall apart as it cooks.

COOK'S TIP

When mixing minced beef with other ingredients the best utensil is your hand — squeeze the meat into the other ingredients until thoroughly combined.

PREPARATION

To roll up the meat in foil:
Carefully slide the meat roll back to the centre of the foil and bring the two short edges of foil together above the roll. Leaving space around the roll, seal the short edges tightly.

CHILLI BEEF LOAF

SERVES 4 · 30 MINS TO PREPARE
1¹/₂ HRS TOTAL TIME·
415 KCAL PER SERVING

700g/1¹/₂lb lean minced beef
15g/¹/₂oz butter
¹/₂ Spanish onion, chopped
50g/2oz fresh white breadcrumbs
225ml/8fl oz tomato ketchup
2 tinned pimentos, drained and diced
2 dried hot red chillies, finely chopped
¹/₂ tsp cayenne pepper
pinch of dried oregano
1 large egg, beaten
salt and freshly ground black pepper
2 chilli flowers, to garnish (optional)
flat-leafed parsley, to garnish (optional)

1 Heat the oven to 180°C/350°F/gas 4. In a small saucepan, heat the butter and sauté the finely chopped onion for 7-10 minutes over a moderate heat, stirring frequently with a wooden spoon, until the onion has softened. Leave to cool a little.

2 Meanwhile, in a large bowl, combine the minced beef, the fresh white breadcrumbs, tomato ketchup, diced pimentos, chopped dried chillies, cayenne pepper, dried oregano, beaten egg and the cooled sautéed onion. Mix together until well blended and season to taste with salt and black pepper.

3 Fill a 1.5L/2¹/₂pt loaf tin with the mixture and level off the top with a palette knife. Place in the oven and bake for 1 hour.

4 Drain the excess fat and turn the meat out onto a heated serving platter, easing it off the sides of the tin with a palette knife, if necessary. Serve at once, garnished with chilli flowers and parsley, if wished.

SERVING IDEAS
A green salad is an excellent accompaniment to this chilli loaf. To complement the strong flavour, add a side dish of Greek yogurt or a bottled sweet chutney.

BEEF & SALAMI RING

THIS MEATY COMBINATION CREATES A TASTY, BUT ECONOMICAL, SUPPER DISH

SERVES 4-6
20 MINS TO PREPARE
1 HR 50 MINS TOTAL TIME
705 KCAL PER SERVING

700g/1½lb minced beef
175g/6oz salami, rind
  removed and
  roughly chopped
100g/4oz fresh white
  breadcrumbs
2 eggs, beaten
4 tsp English mustard
2 tbls tomato purée
1 tsp Worcestershire sauce
½ tsp ground allspice
salt and freshly ground
  black pepper
vegetable oil, for greasing
1 bunch watercress, to
  garnish

1 Heat the oven to 180°C/350°F/gas 4. Brush a 900g/2lb ovenproof ring mould all over with oil.

2 In a large bowl, thoroughly mix together all the ingredients except the oil and watercress. Press the mixture into the prepared ring mould and cover with greased foil. Place on a baking sheet and bake in the oven for about 1¼ hours, or until the loaf is shrinking from the sides of the mould and the juices run clear when the loaf is pierced with a fine skewer.

3 Remove from the oven, leave to settle for about 5 minutes, then run a sharp knife around the edge of the mould and invert a serving plate on top. Hold the mould and plate firmly together and invert them, giving a sharp shake halfway round. Carefully lift the mould off the beef and salami ring.

4 Fill the centre of the ring with watercress sprigs and serve. This dish can be served hot with a tomato or barbecue sauce, or cold with a variety of salads.

BUYING GUIDE
Buy the salami in a piece, rather than sliced, as this makes it easier to skin and chop.

TOMATO-TOPPED MEATLOAF

SERVES 6
20 MINS TO PREPARE
1³/4 HRS TOTAL TIME
330 KCAL PER SERVING

1 tbls sunflower oil
1 onion, chopped
1 garlic clove, crushed
1 celery stick, finely chopped
1 small green pepper,
   deseeded and finely
   chopped
900g/2lb lean minced beef
2 slices brown bread,
   crumbed in a food
   processor or blender
1 egg, beaten
1 tbls Worcestershire sauce
1 tsp dried oregano
salt and freshly ground black
   pepper
450g/1lb baby onions, peeled

TOMATO TOPPING
225ml/8fl oz tin of passata
1 tbls soft light brown sugar
1 tsp wine vinegar
1 tbls wholegrain mustard

1 Heat the oven to 180°C/ 350°F/gas 4. Grease a 900g/ 2lb ring mould. Heat the oil in a heavy-based frying pan. Add the onion, garlic, celery and pepper and cook for about 10 minutes or until soft.

2 Put the mixture in a large bowl. Add the minced beef, breadcrumbs, egg, Worcestershire sauce and oregano. Season with salt and black pepper to taste and mix together well.

3 Spoon the mixture into the prepared mould, pressing it down well and smoothing the surface with the back of a spoon. Bake in the oven for 1 hour. Pour away any fat that may have risen to the surface, then turn the meatloaf out into a baking tray.

4 Put the baby onions in a saucepan of boiling water over low heat and cook for 10 minutes or until the onions are just tender. Drain and set aside.

5 Mix the passata, soft light brown sugar and wine vinegar together in a bowl, then spread 3 tbls of the mixture over the top and sides of the meatloaf. Return to the oven and bake for a further 30 minutes. Remove the meatloaf from the oven and put it on a serving plate.

6 Stir the mustard into the remaining sauce and heat through. Turn the onions in the sauce, then pile them into the centre of the meatloaf. Serve any remaining sauce separately. Serve this meatloaf hot or cold, cut into slices.

MEATLOAF IN SHIRTSLEEVES

SERVES 6 · 1¼ HRS TO PREPARE · 4¾ HRS TOTAL TIME
WITH COOLING · 395 KCAL PER SERVING

15g/½ oz butter, plus extra for greasing
1 Spanish onion, very finely chopped
3 slices stale white bread
75-150ml/3-5fl oz beef stock
225g/½lb minced beef
225g/½lb minced pork
2 tbls parsley, finely chopped
1 tsp Worcestershire sauce
dash of Tabasco sauce or cayenne pepper
salt and freshly ground black pepper
225g/½lb puff pastry
4 tbls French mustard
beaten egg, to glaze
1 bottle fresh tomato sauce
parsley sprigs, to garnish

1 Heat the oven to 220°C/425°F/gas 7. Melt the butter in a heavy-based frying pan and sauté the onion until soft. Trim the bread of crusts. Soak the slices in a little beef stock; then squeeze out as much liquid as possible.

2 In a large bowl, combine the sautéed onion and soaked bread with the minced beef and pork, chopped parsley, Worcestershire sauce, and Tabasco to taste. Mix until smoothly blended, adding seasoning to taste. Grease an 850ml/1½pt loaf tin with butter. Pack the meat mixture into it firmly and level off the top with a spatula. Cover with foil. Bake the meatloaf for 45 minutes. Remove it from the oven and leave to become quite cold.

3 When ready to proceed, heat the oven to 200°C/400°F/gas 6. Roll out the puff pastry into a 30cm/12in square. Turn the meatloaf out of its tin; scrape off any excess fat and spread the loaf with French mustard.

4 Set the loaf in the centre of the pastry square and wrap it like a parcel. Brush the seams with water; seal tightly and trim away the excess pastry. Use the scraps to make a lattice of strips over the top. Brush the pastry with beaten egg and cut small vents on top to let steam escape.

5 Place the wrapped meatloaf on an ungreased baking sheet. Bake for 30 minutes until pastry is puffed and golden. Serve hot garnished with parsley and accompanied by tomato sauce.

BEEFBURGER PARCELS

MAKES 4 · 40 MINS TO PREPARE·
1 HR 10 MINS TOTAL TIME · 610 KCAL PER SERVING

450g/1lb minced beef
salt and freshly ground black pepper
400g/13oz puff pastry
100 g/4 oz smooth chicken liver pâté
1 egg, lightly beaten

1 Heat the oven to 220°C/425°F/gas 7. Season the mince well, then divide it into four equal portions. Shape each into a pattie. Heat a lightly oiled frying pan. When it begins to smoke put in the patties. Cook for 4 minutes on each side, then set aside.

2 Roll out the pastry on a floured surface to a 35cm/14in square then, using a saucer, cut it into four rounds so that each is about 4cm/1½in larger all round than the cooked beefburger. Reserve the pastry trimmings.

3 Spread a quarter of the pâté on top of each beefburger and place pâté side down on the pastry rounds. Brush the pastry edges with water and draw them together over the meat to form a neat parcel. Seal the edges carefully.

4 Dampen a baking sheet and place the parcels on it with their seams underneath. Makes leaves from the pastry trimmings, brush them underneath with water and place them on top of the parcels.

5 Brush the pastry all over with beaten egg. Make two slits in the top of each for the steam to escape and bake in the oven for 15-20 minutes until golden and well risen. Serve hot.

MINCE & POTATO ROLL

SERVES 4 · ³/4 HR TO PREPARE · 3¹/4 HRS TOTAL TIME
WITH COOLING · 450 KCAL PER SERVING

700g/1½lb potatoes
salt and freshly ground
** black pepper**
75g/3oz margarine
1 egg, beaten
350g/12oz minced beef
1 small onion, chopped

1 green pepper,
** deseeded and chopped**
1 tbls tomato ketchup
1 tsp dried mixed herbs
margarine, for greasing
plain flour, for dusting
sweet paprika (optional)

1 Heat the oven to 180°C/350°F/gas 4. Grease a baking tray. Bring the potatoes to the boil in salted water, lower the heat and cook for 20 minutes until tender. Drain, then mash with 50g/2oz margarine. Beat in the egg and season to taste. Refrigerate for 30-60 minutes.

2 Mix the beef, onion, pepper, ketchup and herbs in a bowl. Season to taste. Sift a little flour over a large sheet of greaseproof paper and spoon the potato on top. With a palette knife, pat the potato to a 30 × 23cm/ 12 × 9in oblong.

3 Spread the beef mixture evenly over the potato within 2.5cm/1in of the edges then, starting at a short end, roll up the mixture like a Swiss roll. Seal potato ends.

4 Using the paper, carefully transfer the roll to the prepared tray. Remove paper. Flake remaining margarine over roll and bake in the oven for 1¹/4 hours, until the potato is golden. Sprinkle the top with paprika, if liked, then serve at once.

GREEK LAMB ROLL

THIS DELICIOUS DISH
CARRIES ALL THE
TRADITIONAL FLAVOURS
OF THE MEDITERRANEAN
SERVES 4 · 20 MINS TO PREPARE
1 HR TOTAL TIME
450 KCAL PER SERVING

225g/¹/₂lb puff pastry
I egg, beaten, to glaze

FILLING
250g/9oz minced lamb
I aubergine, weighing about
  250g/9oz, finely chopped
I garlic clove, crushed
25g/Ioz fresh white
  breadcrumbs
I egg, beaten
¹/₂ tsp dried oregano or
  mixed herbs
I tsp chopped fresh mint
¹/₄ tsp freshly grated nutmeg
50g/2oz feta cheese, crumbled
salt and freshly ground black
  pepper

I Heat the oven to 200°C/400°F/gas 6. To make the filling, mix together all the ingredients for the filling except the cheese. Season with salt and pepper to taste.

2 Roll the pastry on a floured surface to make a 33 x 18cm/ 13 x 7in rectangle. Reserve the trimmings.

3 Spoon half of the lamb mixture down the centre of the pastry to within 2.5cm/Iin of the two short ends. Sprinkle the cheese on top and cover with the remaining lamb mixture, Brush the edges of the pastry with water. Seal the two long edges down the length of the loaf, then tuck in the short ends and seal.

4 Dampen a baking sheet and place the roll, sealed side down, on it. Brush with egg and cut two slits on top to let out the steam.

5 Make decorations from the pastry trimmings, brush undersides with water and arrange them on the loaf. Brush all over with beaten egg. Bake in the oven for 35-40

minutes until the filling is cooked through and the pastry is golden, covering the top with foil or greaseproof paper if it begins to overbrown.

6 Transfer to a warmed serving plate and serve hot or cold. This Greek lamb roll can be served with gravy or a tomato sauce.

COOK'S TIPS
The flavour of the dish is best if the aubergine is not peeled. For a less chewy texture, blanch the aubergine for 5 minutes before chopping it.

BUYING GUIDE
Minced lamb is usually sold in supermarkets. Otherwise, ask your butcher to mince lamb for you as most butchers will supply it only on request. Minced beef can be used as an alternative if lamb is difficult to obtain.

WRAPPING IT UP

FROM THE PASTIES OF ENGLAND TO THE TACOS OF MEXICO AND THE SAMOSAS OF INDIA, COOKS AROUND THE WORLD HAVE CREATED EXCITING COMBINATIONS OF MEAT AND PASTRY. FOR THE CALORIE-CONSCIOUS COOK, VEGETABLE WRAPPINGS MAKE A HEALTHIER ALTERNATIVE

MINCE ROLLS

MAKES 24 · 15 MINS TO PREPARE
1 HR 25 MINS TOTAL TIME WITH CHILLING
150 KCAL PER ROLL

50g/2oz fine fresh brown breadcrumbs
225g/¹/₂lb minced pork
50g/2oz Caerphilly cheese, finely grated
1 onion, finely chopped
4 tbls fresh parsley, finely chopped
1 tbls Dijon mustard
2 eggs, beaten
1 extra egg yolk
salt and freshly ground black pepper
flour for dusting
350g/12oz puff pastry

1 Mix the breadcrumbs, meat, cheese, onion and parsley. In another bowl, beat the mustard, half the beaten eggs and the extra egg yolk, then stir this into the meat mixture. Beat well to blend, then season to taste.

2 On a lightly floured surface, roll the pastry to a rectangle approximately 45 x 25cm/18 x 10in. Cut in half lengthways. Divide the filling in half and place each portion on a pastry strip. Shape each portion of filling into long log shapes about 25mm/1in thick in diameter.

3 Brush the pastry edges with some of the egg. Fold each pastry strip in half lengthways to enclose the filling completely. Press the long edges of the pastry together to seal. Trim the ends, then cut each roll into 12 slices, each slice about 4cm/1½in wide. Put the rolls on a plate, cover with clingfilm and chill for at least 30 minutes.

4 Meanwhile, heat the oven to 200°C/400°F/gas 7. Arrange the sausage rolls on a baking sheet. Brush the top of each with the leftover beaten egg, then lightly sprinkle the baking sheet with water.

5 Bake the rolls for 35-40 minutes until the filling is cooked through and the pastry is golden brown. Cover the top with foil or greaseproof paper if it begins to overbrown. Transfer to a wire rack and leave to cool slightly. Serve hot or at room temperature.

6 Serve with cucumber and carrot sticks. A green salad also makes an excellent accompaniment.

MINCE PUFFS

SERVES 4 · 30 MINS TO PREPARE
1 HR TOTAL TIME · 440 KCAL PER SERVING

15g/¹/₂oz butter
125g/4oz bacon rashers, finely diced
225g/¹/₂lb minced beef
50g/2oz mushrooms, finely chopped
1 tbls chopped parsley
celery salt (optional)
freshly ground black pepper
250g/9oz puff pastry
1 egg, beaten
1-2 tbls sesame seeds

1 Melt the butter in a frying-pan over medium heat, add the bacon and mince and fry for 2-3 minutes. Add mushrooms and cook for 5 minutes. Stir in the parsley and season with celery salt, if using, and pepper to taste.

2 Heat the oven to 200°/400°F/gas 6. Roll out the pastry to a square, 30cm/12in. Trim the edges, then cut into 16 squares 7.5cm/3in each. Put meat mixture in the centre of each.

3 Brush the edges with egg. Fold the pastry carefully into triangles, keeping the filling away from the edges. Seal the edges. Brush all the puffs with egg and sprinkle sesame seeds over them. Place the triangles on a dampened baking tray. Bake for 10-15 minutes until the pastry is puffy and golden. Cool the puffs slightly on a wire rack before serving.

PORK PASTIES

SERVES 4 · 30 MINS TO PREPARE
1 HR TOTAL TIME · 560 KCAL PER PASTY

400g/13oz shortcrust pastry
175g/6oz minced pork
1 onion, finely chopped
1 dessert apple, peeled,
  cored and chopped
½ tsp dried thyme
salt and freshly ground black pepper
1 beaten egg, to glaze
vegetable oil for greasing

1 Heat the oven to 200°C/400°F/gas 6. Mix together the pork, onion, apple, thyme and seasoning to taste. Stir well. On a lightly floured surface, roll the pastry into a large round, then, using a 15cm/6in plate as a guide, cut four pastry circles. Divide the filling between the four circles, placing it in the centre of each.

2 Brush the edges of the pastry with beaten egg. Pull the sides up over the filling and seal them firmly together. Flute the edges. Prick the pastry around the top of the pasties to allow steam to escape while they are baking.

3 Put the pasties on a baking sheet and brush with the beaten egg. Bake for 20 minutes, then lower the oven to 180°C/350°F/gas 4. Continue cooking for a further 10 minutes until golden brown. Serve hot, or leave to cool on a wire rack and serve cold. Hot or cold, serve with a selection of relishes or pickled onions.

BEEF & BEAN TURNOVER

SERVES 6 · 35 MINS TO PREPARE
1 HRS 20 MINS TOTAL TIME · 600 KCAL PER TURNOVER

450g/1lb shortcrust pastry	**1 tsp dried thyme**
350g/12oz minced beef	**salt and freshly ground**
2 tbls Worcestershire	**black pepper**
sauce	**225g/8oz tin baked**
1 tbls tomato purée	**beans in tomato sauce**
1 onion, finely chopped	**1 beaten egg, to glaze**
2 tbls chopped parsley	

1 Heat the oven to 180°C/350°F/gas 4. Stir the beef in a bowl with the Worcestershire sauce, tomato purée, onion, herbs and salt and pepper to taste. Fold in the beans carefully; do not crush them.

2 Divide the pastry into 6 pieces. On a floured board roll each into 18cm/7in rounds. Lay a portion of the filling to one side of each round. Brush the edges of the pastry with water, fold the pastry over the filling. Press the edges firmly together to seal them.

3 Place the turnovers on floured baking sheets and brush them with the beaten egg. Prick each turnover four times with a fork so that steam can escape and they do not burst, and place them in the oven. Bake for 45 minutes or until golden brown. Serve hot or cold.

STUFFED SAMOSAS

SERVES 6 · 25 MINS TO PREPARE · 1½ HRS TOTAL TIME,
WITH COOLING · 350 KCAL PER SERVING

DOUGH
175g/6oz plain flour
pinch of salt
4 tbls ghee (or clarified butter)
125ml/4fl oz natural yogurt

FILLING
2 tbls vegetable oil
1 onion, finely chopped
1cm/½in piece of fresh root ginger
  peeled and chopped
1 garlic clove, chopped
2 red or green chillies, finely chopped
1 tsp hot chilli powder
½ tsp turmeric
½ tsp ground coriander
½ tsp salt
225g/8oz minced beef
1 tomato, blanched, peeled and chopped
2 tbls lime or lemon juice

1 To make the dough, mix the flour and salt in a bowl. Make a well in the centre and add 3 tablespoons ghee and yogurt. Draw the flour into the liquid and mix into a soft dough. Turn on to a lightly floured board. Knead for 1 minute. Put the dough in an oiled polythene bag and leave for 30 minutes.

2 To make the filling, heat the oil in a frying pan. When it is hot, add the onion, ginger, garlic and chillies and fry, stirring occasionally, until the onion is soft. Stir in the spices and salt and fry for a further 3 minutes, stirring constantly. Add the beef and fry for 5 minutes. Add the remaining filling ingredients and cook for 5 minutes. Set aside.

3 Roll the dough very thinly. Cut into strips, about 6.5 × 19cm/2½ × 7½in. Brush the edges with milk. Place a little of the filling mixture at the bottom of the strip. Fold over the bottom corner. Continue folding corner to corner to form a multi-layered triangle. Press edges firmly together to seal.

4 Fill a deep-fat fryer two-thirds full with oil and heat until a small cube of bread browns in 40 seconds. Fry the samosas a few at a time until golden brown on each side. Drain on absorbent kitchen towels and serve hot.

BEEF TORTILLAS

TASTY TORTILLAS ARE FILLED WITH SPICY MINCED BEEF, TOMATOES AND ONIONS TO MAKE THIS TRADITIONAL MEXICAN DISH

SERVES 6
20 MINS TO PREPARE
55 MINS TOTAL TIME
325 KCAL PER TORTILLA

12 warm tortillas

FILLING
450g/1lb minced beef
2 tbls vegetable oil
1 onion, finely chopped
1 garlic clove, crushed
225g/8oz tin tomatoes
2 tsp chilli powder
$\frac{1}{2}$ tsp ground cumin
$\frac{1}{2}$ tsp dried oregano
salt

1 To make the beef filling, heat the oil in a frying pan, add the onion and fry gently for 5 minutes until soft and transluscent. Add the garlic and continue to fry for a further 2 minutes.

2 Add the beef and fry briskly, stirring with a wooden spoon to remove any lumps, for about 5 minutes until the meat is evenly browned.

3 Stir in the tomatoes with their juice, the chilli powder, cumin, oregano and salt to taste. Bring to the boil,

then lower the heat and simmer, stirring, for about 20 minutes until the meat is cooked.

4 To serve: spoon a little beef filling into each tortilla, add any extra fillings, then fold over and eat with your fingers.

SERVING SUGGESTIONS
Provide side bowls of shredded lettuce, grated cheese, guacamole (avocado dip), finely chopped onion and bottled taco sauce or any other hot chilli sauce, to the beef filling before folding.

INGREDIENTS GUIDE
Tortillas can be bought ready-made from large supermarkets. To serve them warm, heat them in a moderate oven 180°C/350°F/Gas 4 for 5 minutes until warmed through.

CHILLI BEAN TACOS

TACOS ARE CRISP SHELLS THAT ARE STUFFED
WITH SAVOURY FILLINGS AND EATEN LIKE
SANDWICHES
SERVES 4-6 · 15 MINS TO PREPARE
1 HR TOTAL TIME · 120 KCAL PER TACO

20 tacos

FILLING
2 large onions, chopped
2 tbls oil
450g/1lb minced beef
225g/8oz tin kidney beans
1 red pepper, deseeded and chopped
2 green chillies, finely chopped
2 tbls tomato purée
9 large tomatoes, skinned and chopped
2 garlic cloves, crushed
salt and freshly ground black pepper
1 crisp lettuce, shredded
225g/8oz cottage cheese

1 To prepare the filling, fry the onion in the oil until it is soft and transparent, then add the minced beef and brown. Transfer to a large saucepan and add the tinned kidney beans, red pepper, chillies, tomato purée, chopped tomatoes, garlic and seasoning to taste. Gently simmer for 45 minutes, stirring occasionally to prevent sticking.

2 To serve, place some shredded lettuce on a large serving plate, add a generous spoonful of the filling to each taco, then place them on the plate and top with the cottage cheese.

INGREDIENTS GUIDE
Like tortillas, tacos can be bought in large supermarkets and are ideal for children. To make this recipe less spicy, omit or reduce the quantity of chillies in the filling.

SAVOURY STUFFED MUSHROOMS

SERVES 4 · 20 MINS TO PREPARE
50 MINS TOTAL TIME · 230 KCAL PER SERVING

**10 large mushrooms, each with a
  diameter of approx 7.5cm/3in**
1 tbls olive oil
1 stick of celery, finely chopped
2 shallots, finely chopped
4 bacon rashers
125g/4oz minced beef
50g/2oz fresh breadcrumbs
1 tbls fresh chopped parsley

1   Heat the oven to 220°C/425°F/gas 7. Wipe clean the mushrooms and remove all the stalks. Set aside 8 of the mushrooms. Chop the stalks and the remaining whole mushrooms.

2   Heat the oil in a large, heavy-based frying pan, then add the celery and shallots. Fry for 2-3 minutes until soft. Snip the bacon into strips and add them to the frying pan along with the minced beef. Continue frying until the meat is cooked, stirring occasionally.

3   Add the chopped mushrooms to the pan and fry until the juices begin to run. Remove the pan from the heat and stir in the breadcrumbs and parsley.

4   Roughly divide the mixture into 8 parts, then spoon on to each of the reserved whole mushrooms. Put the stuffed mushrooms in a shallow baking tray and bake for 10-15 minutes. Serve at once while the mushrooms are still hot.

STUFFED ONIONS

SERVES 4 · 30 MINS TO PREPARE
1¾HRS TOTAL TIME · 160 KCAL PER SERVING

4 Spanish onions, peeled
25g/1oz butter
**125g/4oz mushrooms,
  chopped**
125g/4oz minced beef

**2tbls fresh white
  breadcrumbs**
**200ml/7fl oz instant
  gravy**
**1 tbls parsley,
  finely chopped**

1   Heat the oven to 180°C/350°F/gas 4. Bring a large saucepan of water to the boil. Blanch the peeled onions for 10 minutes in the boiling water. Drain, rinse under cold running water, drain again, then remove and discard the outside layer of flesh. Place 1 onion at a time on a tea towel, so that the onion does not slip, and carefully cut out as much of the centre as possible. Repeat with the remaining onions.

2   Chop the centres finely. In a saucepan, heat the butter and sauté the finely chopped onion, the prepared mushrooms and the minced beef over a moderate heat for 7-10 minutes, or until soft. Remove the pan from the heat.

3   Stir in the breadcrumbs and season to taste. Spoon the mixture into the cavities of the hollowed onions, piling the filling high. Make up the instant gravy according to packet instructions. Place the stuffed onions in a heatproof casserole with a tight-fitting lid. Pour the gravy in down the side of the dish. Cover and bake for 1¼hrs until the onions are tender. Sprinkle the onions with finely chopped parsley and serve at once.

PORK-STUFFED CABBAGE LEAVES

IN THIS TYPICAL HUNGARIAN DISH, SAVOY CABBAGE
LEAVES ENCLOSE A ZESTY PORK AND RICE STUFFING
FLAVOURED WITH PAPRIKA, LEMON ZEST AND DILL

SERVES 4 · 20 MINS TO PREPARE
1¼HR TOTAL TIME · 510 KCAL PER SERVING

1 large Savoy cabbage
2 tbls grated onion
1 small carrot, grated
1 garlic clove, chopped
175g/6oz cooked
  long-grain rice
225g/½lb minced pork
grated zest of 1 lemon
1 egg, lightly beaten
2 tsp paprika
½ tsp dill seeds
salt
225g/8oz smoked pork,
  thickly sliced
450ml/¾pt chicken stock

SAUCE
40g/1½oz butter
1½ tbls flour
200ml/7fl oz sour cream
salt and freshly ground pepper

1 Remove 8 large leaves from the Savoy cabbage, taking care not to tear them. Using a small, sharp knife, shave off the thickest part of the stalk to make the leaves easier to roll. Plunge them into boiling water for 2 minutes, then drain under cold running water and pat them dry with kitchen towels.

2 Combine the onion, carrot, garlic, rice and minced pork in a large bowl. Stir in the lemon zest, egg, paprika and dill. Season with salt and mix well. Divide the stuffing between the cabbage leaves. Fold over the bottom, then the sides of each leaf, and roll them up to make a neat parcel.

3 Place the smoked pork slices in the bottom of a heavy-based casserole. Put the cabbage rolls on top, seam side down, and pour over the stock. Bring to the boil on the hob, then cover and simmer for 45-55 minutes over low heat until the cabbage leaves are just tender.

4 Using a slotted spoon, transfer the cabbage rolls to a serving dish. Strain the cooking juices and reserve. Arrange the pork on the serving dish with the cabbage rolls and keep warm.

5 Melt the butter in a small pan, add the flour and stir over low heat for 3 minutes. Increase the heat and gradually stir in 150ml/5fl oz of the reserved cooking juices. Gradually stir in the cream, whisking constantly until the sauce boils and thickens.

6 Simmer over low heat for 3-4 minutes, stirring frequently. Season with salt and pepper to taste. Pour the sauce over the cabbage rolls.

STUFFED AUBERGINES WITH LAMB

ROSEMARY, CINNAMON AND RAISINS LEND A MIDDLE EASTERN FLAVOUR TO THIS DISH

SERVES 4 · 20 MINS TO PREPARE
1 HRS 40 MINS TOTAL TIME · 370 KCAL PER SERVING

2 aubergines
salt and freshly ground black pepper
I tbls olive oil, plus extra for greasing
I onion, chopped
2 garlic cloves, crushed
I tsp ground cinnamon
2 tsp dried rosemary
450g/1lb minced lamb
225g/½lb tin chopped tomatoes
I tbls tomato purée
100g/4oz raisins
100g/4oz long-grain rice, cooked

1 Cut the aubergines in half lengthways and slash the flesh deeply, then sprinkle generously with salt. Place upside down in a colander and leave for 30 minutes to drain away all the bitter juices.

2 Heat the oven to 180°C/350°F/gas 4. Heat the oil in a frying pan over medium heat. Add the onion and garlic and cook for 5 minutes or until softened, stirring frequently. Sprinkle in the cinnamon and rosemary and cook for 2 minutes, stirring..

3 Add the minced lamb, using a spatula to break it up. Fry until brown, stirring often. Stir in the tomatoes and their juice and the tomato purée and mix well, then stir in the raisins and rice and season to taste.

4 Meanwhile, rinse the aubergines and pat dry with kitchen towels. Using a pointed spoon, scoop out the flesh from the centre of each aubergine half, leaving a 6mm/¼in shell. Chop the flesh and stir into the lamb mixture. Simmer for 10 minutes.

5 Spoon the lamb mixture into the aubergine shells. Place in a greased ovenproof dish large enough to take them in a single layer. Add 12mm/½in water. Cover the dish with foil and bake for 1 hour, removing the foil for the last 30 minutes, or until the aubergine shells are tender when pierced. Serve hot or at room temperature.

GREEK-STYLE PEPPERS

SERVES 4 · 25 MINS TO PREPARE
1 HR 25 MINS TOTAL TIME · 345 KCAL PER SERVING

I tbls olive oil	I tbls chopped fresh
I small onion, chopped	thyme
I garlic clove, crushed	I tbls chopped parsley
450g/1lb minced lamb	4 green peppers, halved
2 tbls long-grain rice,	vertically and seeded
cooked and drained	400g/14oz tin chopped
2 tbls tomato purée	tomatoes
I tsp coriander	50g/2oz feta cheese

1 Heat the oven to 190°C/375°F/gas 5. Heat the oil in a heavy-based frying pan and cook the onion and garlic gently for 5 minutes. Add the minced lamb and continue cooking until the meat has lost its pinkness.

2 Stir in the rice, tomato purée, coriander and herbs, adding salt and pepper to taste.

3 Spoon the filling into the pepper halves and arrange in a large, shallow ovenproof dish. Pour the chopped tomatoes around the peppers and crumble the feta cheese over the top.

4 Cover with a lid or tin foil and place in the oven for about 1 hour until the peppers are just tender. Serve at once with additional rice or, more simply, with chunks of wholewheat or French bread.

STUFFED BAKED POTATOES

SERVES 4 · 20 MINS TO PREPARE
1½ HRS TOTAL TIME· 300 KCAL PER SERVING

4 large potatoes	I tsp Worcestershire
I onion, finely chopped	sauce
25g/1oz butter	½tsp dried oregano
150g/6oz minced beef	or marjoram
75g/3oz Cheddar	salt and freshly ground
cheese, grated	black pepper

1 Heat the oven to 190°C/375°F/Gas 5. Scrub the potatoes, pat dry and prick all over with a fork. Bake the potatoes for 1–1¼ hours, or until they are soft.

2 Meanwhile, sauté the onion in the butter for 4–5 minutes, add the beef and sauté over low heat for 5 minutes. Stir in 50g/2oz of the cheese, the Worcestershire sauce and herbs, and season to taste. Mix well and keep hot.

3 Heat the grill to hot. Cut a thin slice from the top of each potato and discard. Scoop out the flesh leaving a shell about 5 mm/¼in thick. Mash the potato flesh and blend thoroughly with the hot meat mixture. Pile back into the potato shells. Sprinkle the tops of the potatoes with the remaining cheese. Place under the grill and cook until the cheese is golden brown.

STUFFED VINE LEAVES

SERVES 4 · 45 MINS TO PREPARE
1¹/2 HRS TOTAL TIME · 480 KCAL PER SERVING

about 40 vine leaves, fresh,
  canned or packaged
2 tbls olive oil
1 small onion, finely chopped
1 garlic clove, crushed
350g/12oz minced lamb
75g/3oz long-grain rice
1 tsp chopped fresh mint,
  or ¹/2 tsp dried mint
1 tbls chopped parsley
225ml/8fl oz chicken stock
salt and freshly ground black pepper
grated zest of ¹/2 lemon
extra oil, for greasing

SAUCE
300ml/¹/2pt tomato juice
150ml/¹/4pt chicken stock
1 tbls lemon juice
1 tbls tomato purée
4 tbls natural yogurt, to garnish

1 If using fresh vine leaves, wash them thoroughly, drain and blanch them in a large pan of boiling water for 1 minute. Drain again, spread the leaves out in a single layer on kitchen towels and pat them dry. If using tinned or packaged vine leaves which have been preserved in brine, put them in a large bowl, pour over boiling water to cover, and leave to soak for 20 minutes. Drain and rinse thoroughly in cold water and pat dry.

2 While the leaves are soaking, heat the oil in a large saucepan, add the onion and garlic and cook over a medium heat for about 5 minutes, until the onion is softened but not brown. Add the lamb and continue to cook, stirring frequently, until it is lightly coloured but not brown. Add the rice and stir for about 2 minutes until it is thoroughly coated and mixed into the lamb.

3 Add the herbs and stock, season to taste with salt and pepper and stir in the lemon zest. Bring the mixture just to the boil, reduce the heat to very low, cover the pan, and simmer for 15 minutes. By this time the rice should have absorbed all the liquid, but the mixture should still be moist. Taste and adjust seasoning if necessary and allow the mixture to cool.

4 Heat the oven to 170°C/325°F/gas 3. Brush a large shallow ovenproof dish with oil. Cover the base of the dish with 8 vine leaves, overlapping them.

5 Take 24 of the remaining vine leaves, place a heaped spoonful of the filling mixture in the centre of each leaf, and roll up the leaves into neat little parcels. Arrange the parcels, seam side downwards, in the prepared dish, placing them close together in a single tightly packed layer.

6 To make the sauce, mix together the tomato juice, stock, lemon juice and tomato purée and season to taste with salt and pepper. Bring the sauce just to the boil in a small saucepan.

7 Pour the sauce over the stuffed vine leaves in the dish. Cover the stuffed vine leaves with the remaining 8 leaves, overlapping so that there are no gaps. Cover the dish with foil.

8 Place the dish in the oven and cook for 50 minutes. To serve, remove foil and top layer of vine leaves from the dish and swirl the yogurt over. Serve at once.

INGREDIENTS GUIDE

If you buy tinned or packaged vine leaves preserved in brine, they are usually rolled or packed very tightly together. A 450g/1lb tin usually contains about 48 leaves, while a 225g/8oz polythene pack contains about 24 leaves.